DISCOVERING LANGUAGES
GERMAN

TEACHER'S EDITION

Elaine S. Robbins
Formerly Mount Logan Middle School
Logan, Utah

Kathryn R. Ashworth
Brigham Young University

AMSCO SCHOOL PUBLICATIONS, INC.
315 Hudson Street / New York, N.Y. 10013

Cassettes

The DISCOVERING LANGUAGES series includes two cassettes for each language, except Latin. The voices are those of native speakers.

Each cassette includes the following material:

Oral exercises in four-phased sequences: cue—pause for student response—correct response by native speaker—pause for student repetition.

The dialogs at normal listening speed.

Questions or completions in four-phased sequences.

Seven or eight songs for each language, sung with accompaniment.

The German cassettes (Ordering Code N 592 C) are available separately from the publisher. A complete cassette script is included.

When ordering this book, please specify R 592 T or DISCOVERING LANGUAGES: GERMAN, TEACHER'S EDITION

ISBN 1-56765-402-9

Copyright © 1995 by Amsco School Publications, Inc.

Songs by Uwe Kind

Printed in the United States of America

2 3 4 5 6 7 8 9 10   02 01 00 99 98 97 96

Preface

DISCOVERING LANGUAGES is a four-color foreign language program consisting of five separate texts: French, German, Italian, Spanish, and Latin. An additional component, *Origins and History of Language,* suitable for reproduction, is an integral part of the program and is included in this Teacher's Edition. DISCOVERING LANGUAGES is designed for either a one-year or one-semester course in upper-elementary or middle-school Foreign Language Exploratory programs, commonly known as FLEX. The DISCOVERING LANGUAGES Program aims to:

➡ Offer students an opportunity to begin communicating in different foreign languages in a formal course before choosing one language for further study.

➡ Foster a global perspective by exposing students to several foreign languages, the countries where they are spoken, and the people who speak them.

➡ Heighten students' appreciation and respect for cultural diversity and sharpen their cross-cultural awareness and sensitivity.

➡ Introduce students to the rich ethnic heritage of the English language and provide them with an insight into the nature of language, its origins and early development, language families, and similarities among languages.

➡ Develop interdisciplinary skills by linking foreign language study with language arts, social studies, and math.

DISCOVERING LANGUAGES is designed to give students the opportunity to begin communicating in a foreign language in a natural, personalized, enjoyable, and rewarding context. Communication is developed through simple materials in visually focused topical contexts.

The text for each language of the DISCOVERING LANGUAGES Program includes an introduction to the specific country, its language and people. A final review section practices and reinforces the vocabulary and culture taught in preceding sections. Illustrated cultural notes offer views and insights into aspects of foreign life that students can easily relate to their own lives.

Each section includes a variety of activities designed to give students the feeling that not only can they learn all that has been presented but that they can also have fun practicing the foreign language. Activities include dialogs in cartoon-strip fashion, picture-cued exercises and puzzles, skits and conversations, coloring activities, songs, and games. The words and expressions, as well as the language structures introduced in DISCOVERING LANGUAGES, have been carefully chosen and limited to insure student comfort and success.

Origins and History of Language

A sixteen-page discussion on the origins and history of language, suitable for reproduction, is included in each Teacher's Edition. It covers prehistoric messages, early systems of writing, early alphabets, languages of Europe; a history of the English language, the Latin-English connection, and information on the richness of language of American place-names. An integral component of DISCOVERING LANGUAGES, this unit provides an interesting introduction to the program.

Vocabulary

Each section begins with topically related illustrations that convey the meanings of new words in the target language without recourse to English. This device enables students to make a direct and vivid association between the foreign terms and their meanings. Most activities use illustrations and picture cues to practice words and expressions.

To facilitate comprehension an early section of each book is devoted to cognates of English words. Beginning a course in this way shows students that the target language is not so "foreign" after all and helps them overcome any fears they may have about the difficulty of learning a language. Words and expressions are limited and structure is simple and straightforward. Because students are not overburdened, they quickly gain a feeling of success.

Conversation

Students learn to express themselves and talk about their families and friends. They learn to greet people, to tell the day and month of the year, to identify and describe people and objects, and more. Skits and conversational activities follow situational dialogs in cartoon-strip style, encouraging students to begin using the target language for communication and self-expression. These activities serve as a springboard for personalized communication in pairs or groups.

Pronunciation

Throughout each book of the series, a lively and often humorous cartoon detective will guide students on how to pronounce the sounds and words of the particular language.

Songs

Each language component, except Latin, includes seven or eight songs in its Teacher's Edition, incorporating much of the vocabulary of the book and providing an amusing and effective learning tool. The songs include numbers, days of the week, colors, parts of the body, and more. Musical arrangements and lyrics, as well as English translations, are provided in the Teacher's Editions and the cassette scripts.

Culture

The first section of each book introduces students to the foreign language, its speakers, and the countries where it is spoken. Illustrated cultural notes follow most sections and offer students a variety of views and insights into well-known and not so well-known aspects of the culture: school, holidays, leisure time, sports, and interesting manners and customs.

Teacher's Editions

The Teacher's Edition for each language provides a wealth of suggestions and strategies for teaching all elements in the book. Also included are supplementary listening and speaking activities, total physical response activities, projects and research topics, and additional cultural information to supplement the cultural notes in the student book. The Teacher's Editions also include musical arrangements and lyrics for the target language songs together with English translations for the songs and a complete Key to all exercises and puzzles.

Cassettes

Two cassettes with a printed script are available from the publisher for each language except Latin. They include oral exercises, questions, completions, and dialogs, all with appropriate pauses for response or repetition. The cassettes also include the songs in the Teacher's Editions, sung with accompaniment.

Teacher Preparation

The DISCOVERING LANGUAGES Program is designed with the foreign-language teacher as well as the non-foreign-language teacher in mind. The simple and straightforward vocabulary and structures taught in the course can be easily mastered by teachers with little knowledge of the target language. Instructors with no knowledge of the foreign language will find the Teacher's Edition and the cassette accompanying each language component particularly useful tools.

Origins and History of Language

1 Prehistoric Messages

About one hundred years ago, river pebbles were discovered under layers of debris in a cave in southern France. These pebbles, untouched for tens of thousands of years, were decorated with lines and dots of a red paint called ocher. The markings resembled a form of writing. What was the purpose of these marked pebbles? Scientists guessed that they were good-luck charms, but no one knew with certainty.

In the early 1960s, the scientist Alexander Marshack discovered prehistoric bones gouged with scratches and marks. He explained these markings as examples of early people's efforts to count, tally, and number objects. Many similar bones have been found since that time.

As early as thirty thousand years ago, cave dwellers in Spain and France told stories about hunting by painting pictures on cave walls. These picture stories are the earliest known examples of "written" ideas. A cave in Altamira, Spain, contains some of the most important examples of cave art. The pictures at Altamira show bisons, wild horses, deer with huge antlers, and strange prehistoric creatures in yellow, red, brown, and black. What inspired these pictures? What was their purpose? Some have guessed that primitive people painted these scenes to bring them luck in the hunt.

For thousands of years, people expressed themselves by drawing, painting, and etching on rocks and other surfaces. Storytelling pictures in caves have been discovered in many areas of the world. From them we have learned much about how prehistoric people built huts, plowed, planted, and performed a variety of other activities. They give us a glimpse into the life and customs of prehistoric people.

Stone markings, cave paintings, and bone decorations are the earliest forms of "written" communication. Although spoken language came before written language, we do not know how prehistoric people spoke. Did they communicate by making animal sounds? For example, did they refer to a cat by making the sound *meow*, and did *meow* then become the word for cat? These and many other questions may never be answered.

Activity A

1. Where and when were pebbles with primitive markings resembling writing discovered?

_____

2. What did the markings mean?

_____

3. Which came first, speaking or writing?

_____

4. How many years ago were animals painted in the cave in Altamira, Spain?

_____

5. What can we learn from cave art?

_____

2 Early Systems of Writing

Over many thousands of years, people invented and discovered ways to improve their lives. They learned to raise crops by using irrigation; they learned to weave cloth, to build houses, chariots, ships with sails; and they developed tools and weapons. They began to live in cities and trade the goods they produced. As life grew more and more complex, it became essential to find a way to record and communicate the ever-increasing amount of information people had to remember. And so people began to write.

The earliest people to develop a form of writing were the Sumerians, who lived in an ancient land called Mesopotamia, known today as Iraq, about five thousand years ago.

The Sumerians advanced far beyond their neighbors because their efficient method of writing replaced complicated pictures or scratches on bones. At first the Sumerians created a system of writing made up of many simplified pictures that stood for words. For example, a crown would mean king, a spear would mean kill, waves would mean sea, and so on. The next step the Sumerians took to make their writing less complicated is the single most important step in the history of writing. To make it easier to understand this important step, let's pretend that the Sumerians spoke English.

At the beginning, Sumerians used one picture for every word in their language. To write the word *sea*—the body of water—they used one picture, 〜〜〜, and to write the verb *to see* they used another picture, 👁 👁 . At a certain point, the Sumerians realized that two different pictures were not necessary to express the same-sounding word. So they began to use one picture for both words. For example, they chose this picture, 〜〜〜 , to write both the words *sea* and *to see*.

With time, they went one step further. They began to use the picture 〜〜〜

whenever the sound *see* occurred WITHIN a word. For the word *season*, for example, they used the symbol 〜〜〜 followed by the symbol for *sun* and wrote *season* like this: 〜〜〜 + ☉ .

If we wrote English using the Sumerian way of writing, this is how we would write the following words:

kitten   starfish

And these sentences would be written as follows:

Aunt saw king.

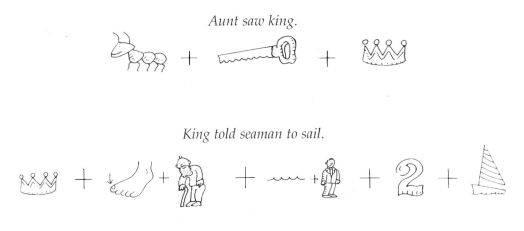

King told seaman to sail.

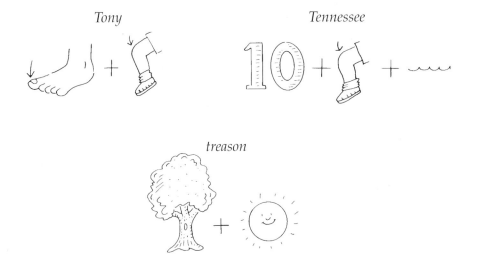

Having picture symbols stand for sounds not only cut down on the thousands of pictures the Sumerians needed to remember but also made it possible to write words that could not be illustrated with a picture, such as names of people, cities, and abstract words. Here are some examples:

Tony

Tennessee

treason

Does this remind you of a game? You have probably played the rebus game. That is exactly how writing began.

Activity B

Now you try. Write the following words using the rebus principle:

1. penmanship _____

2. horseshoe _____

3. many _____

4. penny _____

5. seesaw _____

6. skinny _____

7. heartless _____

8. heartburn _____

9. tighten _____

10. timeless _____

11. cowboy _____

12. kitten _____

3 Early Alphabets

In order to write in ancient Sumerian, hundreds of symbols had to be memorized and the symbols had to be carefully written. Since it was difficult for everyone to learn so many symbols, writing became the job of a small number of people called scribes. In time, scribes improved and simplified the symbols of the written language in order to make their work easier.

It took the Sumerians a long time to come up with an efficient and accurate writing system known as cuneiform. The Sumerians pressed their writing instruments into clay tablets while the clay was damp and soft. Some of their neighbors—the Babylonians, the Assyrians, and the Persians—borrowed the idea of writing from the Sumerians and adapted it to the sounds of their own languages.

The ancient Egyptians developed a different writing system. Like the Sumerians, they also used symbols and signs that stood for words and parts of words, but they created symbols called hieroglyphs. They wrote on papyrus scrolls instead of clay tablets. Papyrus was a paperlike material made from the fibers of reeds that grew along the Nile River.

The next important step in the history of writing was taken by the Phoenicians, who lived along the easternmost coast of the Mediterranean Sea. They realized the value of writing but found the picture writing of the Egyptians complicated and awkward. Instead, the Phoenicians developed a system of only 22 to 30 symbols. This system was not like the Sumerian and Egyptian writing systems where a picture symbol stood for a whole word or part of a word. In the Phoenician writing system, one symbol stood for a single consonant plus a vowel sound.

The alphabet was the next step. When the Greeks started using separate symbols for vowels and consonants, the first true alphabet was created.

The alphabet developed by the Greeks was to become the foundation of the Roman alphabet, which is very similar to the one we use today. The Greeks also gave us the word *alphabet*. *Alpha* is the first letter of the Greek alphabet, and *beta* is the second.

Now compare the different writing systems illustrated on page *xiii*. Note that the Egyptian symbols date back to 3000 B.C., the Phoenician symbols to 1000 B.C., the Greek alphabet to 600 B.C., and the Roman alphabet to A.D. 114. Capital letters were the only forms used in the Greek and Roman alphabets. Lower-case letters developed gradually from the small letters used by scribes who needed to fit more words in the books they copied by hand.

The Roman alphabet closely resembles our modern alphabet except for the letters *J, U*, and *W*, which were added to the alphabet during the Middle Ages.

Egyptian	Phoenician	Greek	Roman
		A	A
		B	B
		Γ	C
		Δ	D
		E	E
		F	F
		Γ	G
		H	H
		I	I
		I	I
		K	K
		Λ	L
		M	M

Egyptian	Phoenician	Greek	Roman
		N	N
		O	O
		Γ	P
		Q	Q
		P	R
		Σ	S
		T	T
		Υ	V
		Υ	V
		Υ	V
		X	X
		Υ	Y
		Z	Z

Activity C

1. Who were the people who made cuneiform writings on clay tablets?

_____

2. What was the name of the land where these people lived?

_____

3. Why did the Sumerians need to invent writing?

_____

4. Did every Sumerian learn cuneiform writing? Why or why not?

_____

5. What was the writing of the ancient Egyptians called?

_____

6. How was Phoenician writing different from hieroglyphics and cuneiform writing?

_____

7. What was the name of the people who invented the true alphabet?

_____

8. Where does the word *alphabet* come from?

_____

4 The Languages of Europe

About three thousand languages are spoken around the world. All these languages have been grouped into nine major families. Language families are groups of languages that are related because they developed from a single common language called the parent language.

Indo-European is the most widespread language family in the world. About half of the world's population today speaks an Indo-European language, including most of the people of modern Europe. All the Indo-European languages came from the same parent language. Although there are no records of the parent language, scientists believe that a very long time ago speakers of this language lived in central Europe. As these people grew in number, they moved into other areas of the European continent and of the world. Some went to the country we now call Greece. Others went to Italy, France, and England. Some moved north to the Baltic countries, and still others went east to Russia. The farthest any of these people are believed to have gone is Asia Minor and northern India.

These groups took their language with them, but once they were separated from one another, the parent language they all spoke began to change. Now, after thousands of years, the language of each group has changed so much that one group cannot understand the other.

The Indo-European family of languages is divided into several smaller groups or subgroups. The following is a partial list of these subgroups and the modern languages that evolved from them:

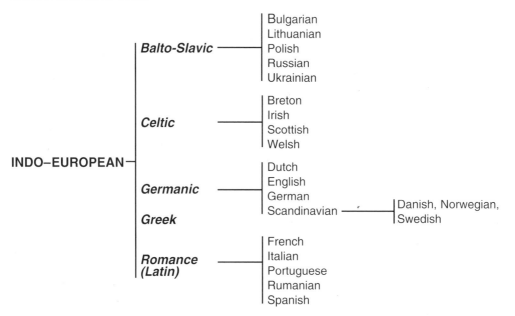

Activity D

Now with your teacher's help, look at a world map and identify those countries whose languages belong to the Indo-European family of languages.

Although the sounds and forms of the original Indo-European parent language have changed, many of its basic words are still found in different modern languages today.

Look at the similarities in these examples:

ENGLISH	LATIN	ITALIAN	FRENCH	SPANISH	GERMAN
circus	circus	circo	cirque	circo	Zirkus
mother	mater	madre	mère	madre	Mutter
nature	natura	natura	nature	naturaleza	Natur
nose	nasus	naso	nez	nariz	Nase
stadium	stadium	stadio	stade	estadio	Stadion

English derived from the Germanic subgroup, but it also contains many words of the Romance subgroup of languages.

The three most widely spoken languages of the Western Hemisphere are English, Spanish, and Portuguese. French, another European language, is also spoken by several million people in eastern Canada and the Caribbean. English, Spanish, Portuguese, and French explorers and settlers were the first Europeans to bring their languages to the New World.

Languages are always changing. As we speak, new words are being created and added to our own English language. Every new discovery in science and technology, for example, requires a new word. Think about it. Did the words *laser* and *compact disc* exist fifty years ago?

New words are also added to English when words are borrowed from other languages. In English, for example, we use the German words **gesundheit** and **pumpernickel,** the French words **ballet** and **boutique,** the Italian words **maestro** and **fiasco,** and the Spanish words **pimiento** and **patio.**

Activity E

1. Name the three leading languages of the Western Hemisphere.

   _____

2. Name a fourth European language, which is spoken in eastern Canada.

   _____

3. What is the name of the language family from which scientists think most European languages came?

   _____

4. Name five modern languages of the Romance language subgroup.

   _____

5. English is a combination of which two language subgroups?

   _____

6. Name five words that have been created and added to English in the last fifty years.

   _____

7. Name five foreign words that English has borrowed from other languages.

   _____

5 History of the English Language

English is the most widely spoken language in the world today. The origins of the English language go way back to a language spoken more than two thousand years ago by people called the Celts, who lived in what is now England.

The history of the English language can be divided into three periods:

1. The Old English period, from 500 to 1000
2. The Middle English period, from 1100 to 1500
3. The Modern English period, from 1500 to the present

During this long span of time, England was invaded and ruled by people from different areas of Europe, each bringing with them their own languages.

First came the Romans who conquered England and ruled over the Celts from 50 B.C. to A.D. 400. Around A.D. 450, three Germanic tribes known as the Jutes, the Angles, and the Saxons invaded England. These tribes brought with them Germanic languages that resemble modern German. With time these languages mixed to form what is called Old English, also known as Anglo-Saxon.

During the mid-1000s, the Normans, a people living in northern France, invaded England. They brought with them the French language of the time. The people of England borrowed thousands of French words and made them part of their own language. The pronunciation and word order of Old English also changed under the influence of the Normans.

In addition to French, a great number of Latin words entered the language spoken in England. Latin was an influential language used by church officials and courts of law. The language that resulted from the mixture of Old English, French, and Latin is called Middle English.

By the sixteenth century, Middle English had changed so much that a person who spoke Old English would not have understood it. Over the next few hundred years, English borrowed words from many different languages and slowly developed into Modern English.

Beginning in the 1600s, the English language began to spread across the world as the English explored and colonized North America, Africa, Australia, and India.

6 The Latin-English Connection

More than half of all English words come from Latin. Some English words are spelled exactly like Latin: **odor, color, circus.** In many other words, the only difference between English and Latin is one or two letters: **machina, natura, familia.**

Here is a list of Latin words and their meanings. Now look at the English word that came from the Latin word. Write the definition of each of the English words in the empty boxes.

LATIN	MEANING	ENGLISH	DEFINITION
agricola	*farmer*	agriculture	
canis	*dog*	canine	
digitus	*finger*	digit	
femina	*woman*	feminine	
lavare	*to wash*	lavatory	
salutare	*to greet*	salute	
venditare	*to sell*	vendor	
laborare	*to work*	laboratory	

Now look at these Latin words and their meanings. Find an English word that comes from the Latin. You may be able to come up with more than one English word. An example is given to get you started.

LATIN	MEANING	ENGLISH WORD(S)
pedis	*foot*	pedal, pedicure, pedestrian
aqua	*water*	
dentis	*teeth*	
libri	*books*	
frigidus	*cold*	
vocabulum	*word*	
spectare	*to watch*	
portare	*to carry*	
lavare	*to wash*	
computare	*to count, do figures*	

Many other English words are often made up of two Latin words. For example, the English word *submarine* comes from the Latin prefix **sub-** meaning "under" and the Latin root (or base) **marinus** meaning "sea." The short Latin word **sub-** is called a prefix because it is placed before the root. Look at how it works:

PREFIX	+	ROOT	=	LITERAL ENGLISH MEANING	ENGLISH WORD
sub-	+	**marinus**	=	*under the sea*	*submarine*

Now you do it. Here is a list of common prefixes + root words and their meanings. Can you combine them to form an English word? Write the literal English meaning and the English word in the empty boxes. Some examples are given to get you started.

PREFIX	+	ROOT	=	LITERAL ENGLISH MEANING	ENGLISH WORD
in- *in, into*	+	**vadere** *to advance*	=	*to advance into*	*invade*
circum- *around*	+	**navigare** *to sail*	=	*to sail around*	*circumnavigate*
ex- *out of, from*	+	**portare** *to carry*	=		
im- *in, into*	+	**portare** *to carry*	=		
trans- *across*	+	**portare** *to carry*	=		
in- *in, into*	+	**habitare** *to live*	=		
intro- *in, inward*	+	**ducere** *to lead*	=		
inter- *between*	+	**rumpere** *to break*	=		
sub- *under*	+	**terrenus** *earth*	=		
suc- *up*	+	**cedere** *to go*	=		
pro *forward*	+	**cedere** *to go*	=		

As you can see, the Latin-English connection is a strong one. If we took a closer look at German and as well as other European languages, we would also find thousands of words that resemble English. By learning a foreign language not only are we able to communicate with and appreciate people from different countries and cultures, we also learn a lot about our own language, English.

7 Language Richness of American Place Names

Spanish Place Names

The Spanish language first came to America in 1492 with Christopher Columbus's expedition. In the following years, Spanish spread across the lands conquered and settled by Spanish explorers.

Many names of American cities, especially in the West, come from Spanish. Las Vegas (Nevada) means "the meadows"; Sacramento (California) means "sacrament"; Pueblo (Colorado) means "town"; and Los Angeles (California) means "the angels." San Francisco is Spanish for "Saint Francis," and San Diego for "Saint James."

There are Spanish place names for states as well. Florida was originally called **Pascua Florida,** Spanish for "flowered Easter." Montana means "mountain." Colorado comes from the Spanish word **colorado** meaning "colored" or "reddish," the color of the Colorado River when it carries a load of silt through the red rock country it crosses.

Many other Spanish place names are found in the East, West, and Southwest. The mountain range between Nevada and California is called the Sierra Nevada, Spanish for "snowy mountain range." The Alamo in Texas is Spanish for "poplar tree," a tree that grew where settlers found water.

Native American Place Names

Native Americans lived in North America before the Spanish, English, or French settled in America. The Mohawks, Oneidas, Onondagas, Cayugas, and Senecas made up the five Iroquois nations of central New York. Many American Indian words remain for states, cities, mountains, and rivers in that area and across the United States. Lakes Michigan, Huron, and Erie, as well as the Mississippi and Missouri rivers, come from Indian names. These names were also given to cities and states. Other states' names that came from the Indians are Illinois, Massachusetts, Minnesota, Alaska, Connecticut, and Utah.

English Place Names

The East Coast of the United States was colonized by the English, and many of its place names are of English origin. The Puritans who sailed on the *Mayflower* named Plymouth after an English city. The cities of Boston, Bristol, Cambridge, Kent, and Lancaster were named after towns and counties in England.

The English also named cities in honor of their kings, queens, and nobility. Jamestown, Virginia, an early colony, is named after King James I. New York is named in honor of the Duke of York, brother of King Charles II.

The names of English explorers are also found on the map of the United States. Henry Hudson sailed up the East Coast and into the river later named in his honor. Pennsylvania honors its founder, the Quaker leader William Penn. Baltimore, Maryland, is named after its founder, Lord Baltimore.

French Place Names

French explorers and settlers also named places after French cities, kings, and explorers. New Orleans is named after the French city of **Orléans** saved by the heroic Joan of Arc, who led the French army against an English invasion. Louisiana was named for King Louis XIV, the king of France when the territory of Louisiana was explored and claimed by French explorers.

Provo, Utah, was named after Étienne Provost, a French-Canadian fur trader. Des Moines, Iowa, means "of the monks" in French and refers to the Catholic missionaries who explored the area. Lake Champlain, in New York, is named for its discoverer, Samuel Champlain.

The French gave many descriptive names to places they discovered or founded. Boise, Idaho, comes from the French word for "woods." Presque Isle, in Pennsylvania, Maine, and Michigan, means "almost an island." Eau Claire, Wisconsin, means "clear water"; Fond du Lac, in Wisconsin and Minnesota, means "far end of the lake"; and Belle Plaine, Iowa, means "beautiful plain."

The word **ville** in French means "city" or "town." As with the word **town** in Jamestown and Englishtown, the word **ville** was added to another word to come up with the name of towns: Knoxville and Nashville in Tennessee; Belleville, La Fargeville, and Depauville in northern New York.

Italian, Greek, Latin, and German Influences

Spanish, English, French, and Indian words are the main sources of names of places in the United States, but there are others. America was named after the Italian explorer Amerigo Vespucci, who determined that the Americas were a separate continent from Asia.

Many American places were named after places and people of ancient Greek and Roman civilizations: Seneca, Ithaca, Carthage, Euclid. Philadelphia means "city of brotherly love" in Greek. Agricola, a town name in several states, means "farmer" in Latin. German settlers gave their new Missouri home a Latin name, Concordia, meaning "concord" or "peace."

Many cities in Pennsylvania end with the word **burg** or **burgh,** German for "castle" or "fort": Pittsburgh, Harrisburg, Strasburg, Mechanicsburg. Gothenburg, in Nebraska, the site of an old Pony Express station, was named for a city in Sweden.

Further Study

We could go on and on with the study of the origins of American place names. The richness and diversity of the population in the United States are evident in the great variety of place names. Remember, early settlers had an enormous new country to name. They used the languages and the names of places they knew. Settlers far away from home probably felt less homesick when surrounded by familiar place names.

When you see the name of a city or a street, a river or a lake, a state or a county, ask yourself what language it may have come from. You may find the origin and story of place names in dictionaries of American place names in your local or school library. Why don't you start by finding the story of the name of your street, city, county, or state?

Activity F

1. List three Spanish place names with their English meanings.

_____

2. Who lived in what is now the United States before any Europeans came?

_____

3. List three states with Indian names.

_____

4. Name three American cities that have been named for places in England.

_____

5. For whom is New York named?

_____

6. What do the French word **ville** and the German word **burg** mean? Can you find two cities in your area that end with **ville** and two that end with **burg?**

_____

7. List three French place names with their English meanings.

_____

8. What language does the name America come from?

_____

Resources and References

History of Language

Beowulf. Trans. Howell D. Chickering, Jr. Garden City, NY: Anchor Press/Doubleday, 1977.

Beowulf. Trans. Charles W. Kennedy. Eleventh Printing. New York: Oxford University Press, 1962.

Cahn, William, and Cahn, Rhoda. *The Story of Writing.* Harvey House, 1963.

Charlin, Remy; Beth, Mary; and Ancona, George. *Handtalk: An ABC of Finger Spelling and Sign Language.* Parents' Magazine Press, 1974.

Chaucer, Geoffrey. *The Riverside Chaucer.* Larry D. Benson, ed. Boston: Houghton Mifflin, 1987.

Davidson, Jessica. *Is That Mother in the Bottle? Where Language Came From and Where It Is Going.* New York: Watts, 1972.

Davidson, Marshall, ed. *Great Civilizations of the Past: Golden Book of Lost Worlds.* New York: Golden Books, 1962.

Epstein, Sam, and Epstein, Beryl. *All About Prehistoric Cave Men.* New York: Random House, 1959.

Ernst, Margaret. *Words: English Roots and How They Grew.* NY: Harper and Row, 1982.

Gannette, Henry. *The Origin of Certain Place Names in the United States.* Detroit: Gale Research Company, 1971.

Harder, Kelsie B. *Illustrated Dictionary of Place Names.* New York: Van Nostrand Reinhold, 1976.

Longman, Harold. *What's Behind the Word?* New York: Perl, Coward-McCann, 1968.

Pei, Mario. *The Story of Language.* Philadelphia: J.B. Lippincott, 1984.

Rogers, Frances. *Painted Rock to Printed Page: History of Printing and Communication.* Philadelphia: Lippincott, 1960.

Scott, Joseph, and Scott, Lenore. *Egyptian Hieroglyphs for Everyone: An Introduction to the Writing of Ancient Egypt.* New York: Funk and Wagnalls, 1968.

The World Book Encyclopedia. Chicago: World Book, Inc., 1994.

Foreign Countries

Balerdi, Susan. *France: The Crossroads of Europe.* Dillon Press, 1984. For younger readers.

Bradley, Catherine. *Germany: The Reunification of a Nation.* Gloucester Press, 1991. For younger readers.

Farfield, Sheila. *Peoples and Nations of Africa.* Gareth Stevens, 1988.

Georges, D.V. *South America.* Children's Press, 1986.

James, Ian. *Italy.* Watts, 1988. For younger readers.

Miller, Arthur. *Spain.* Chelsea House, 1988. For younger readers.

Resources and References *(continued)*

Filmstrips

Ancient Civilizations. National Geographic Society.
Christmas in France. Huntsville, TX: Educational Filmstrips.
Christmas in Germany. Huntsville, TX: Educational Filmstrips.
Christmas in Spain. Huntsville, TX: Educational Filmstrips.
France. Huntsville, TX: Educational Filmstrips.
Germany, West and East. Niles, IL: United Learning.
Glimpses of West Africa. Gessler Publishing Co.
Let's Visit Mexico. Pleasantville, NY: EAV.
Let's Visit South America. Pleasantville, NY: EAV.
Let's Visit Spain. Pleasantville, NY: EAV.
Martinique et Guadeloupe. Gessler Publishing Co.

Pedagogy

Curtain, A., and Pesola, Ann C. *Languages and Children—Making the Match.* Addison-Wesley, 1988.

Kennedy, D., and De Lorenzo, W.E. *Complete Guide to Exploratory Foreign Language Programs.* Lincolnwood, IL: National Textbook Company, 1985.

Raven, P.T. *FLEX: A Foreign Language Experience.* ERIC Document No. ED 238 301, 1983.

Seelye, H. Ned. *Teaching Culture.* Lincolnwood, IL: National Textbook Co., 1984.

Dictionaries

(All Amsco School Publications, New York)

The New College French & English Dictionary, 1988.
The New College German & English Dictionary, 1981.
The New College Italian & English Dictionary, 1976.
The New College Latin & English Dictionary, 1994.
The New College Spanish & English Dictionary, 1987.

To the Student

You are about to embark on a journey of discovery — beginning to learn a new language spoken by millions of people around the world, GERMAN.

Learning German provides an opportunity to explore another language and culture. German may be one of several languages you will discover in this course. You can then select which language you will continue to study.

Whatever your goals, this book will be a fun beginning in exploring a special gift you have as a human being: the ability to speak a language other than your own. The more you learn how to communicate with other people, the better you will be able to live and work in the world around you.

In this book, you will discover the German language and the world where it is spoken. The German words and expressions you will learn have been limited so that you will feel at ease.

You will learn how to express many things in German: how to greet people, how to count, how to tell the day and month of the year, how to identify and describe many objects, and more.

You will use German to talk about yourself and your friends. You will practice with many different activities, like puzzles and word games, German songs, fun cartoons, and pictures. Some activities you will do with classmates or with the whole class. You will act out skits and conversations and sing German songs. You will learn about many interesting bits of German culture: school days, holidays, school and leisure time, sports, and interesting manners and customs.

You will also meet young Udo, who will be your guide on how to pronounce German words. Look for Udo's clues throughout this book and get a feel for the German language, its sounds, and its musical quality. You will also develop an ear for German, so listen carefully to your teacher and the cassettes.

You will quickly realize that learning a new language is not as hard as you might have imagined. Enjoy using it with your teacher and classmates. Try not to be shy or afraid of making mistakes when speaking: remember, the more you speak, the more you will learn. And you can even show off the German you learn to family, relatives, and friends. After all, learning a new language means talking with the rest of the world and with each other.

Now — on to German. **Viel Glück!**, which means *Good luck!*

— *K.R.A.*

Contents

Germany and the German Language

1

NOTE TO TEACHERS

➡ Be sure not to rush through the introduction or the cultural sections, **Kulturwinkel.** Students are always intrigued by foreign lands and cultures. They ask many questions about cultural differences and remember cultural details long after they may have forgotten language and grammatical points.

➡ Take time to study the art and maps in the book and supplement the text with postcards and magazines, travel brochures, posters, souvenirs and artifacts, slides and photographs, and video materials. You may have students find some of these materials themselves. Relatives, friends, libraries, travel agencies, consulates, and cultural entities are excellent sources for students to contact. Set up a classroom bulletin board or have students create collages in the shape of Germany, Austria, Switzerland, or Liechtenstein, on which to display postcards, photos, and so on.

➡ Students also love to hear personal stories and anecdotes. If possible, provide authentic and personalized information about German-speaking countries and culture by relating your own stories or inviting a native or someone who has visited a German-speaking country to speak to students and answer questions.

Kulturwinkel (Supplementary Culture)

➡ The German Empire was founded by Charlemagne in the 800s and was made up of what is today France, Germany, and the northern half of Italy. After Charlemagne's death in 843, his empire was divided into three kingdoms, one for each of his grandsons: lands east of the Rhine River, later to become what is now Germany; the western lands, later called France; and the central lands, most of which is now Italy. Germany received its name from the Romans, who called it **Germania.**

➡ Although Germany's southern border falls on the same latitude as Quebec or Seattle, the whole country enjoys a moderate climate thanks to prevailing westerly winds that bring warmth from the Atlantic Ocean. Temperatures rarely fall below 30°F in winter or rise above 75°F in summer.

➡ About one-fourth of Germany is covered with forests. The most important, the Black Forest, is situated in the southwestern corner of the country.

➡ Germany is one of the most densely populated countries in Europe, with 80 percent of its people living in urban areas. Slightly smaller than the state of Montana, Germany has a population of 81 million. The major cities are Berlin, its capital and largest city, Hamburg, Munich, Frankfurt, Cologne, and Stuttgart. Many German cities were destroyed during World War II and rebuilt during the 1950s and 1960s.

➡ Germany is one of the world's most advanced industrial nations and its people enjoy one of the highest standards of living in Europe. The most important manufacturing products are chemicals, steel, machinery, automobiles, textiles, and beer. German farms do not supply enough food for the needs of the country; as a result, it imports much of its food.

Germany **(Deutschland),** slightly smaller than the state of Montana, is one of the largest countries in western Europe. Northern Germany is low and flat, sloping upwards to the central highlands and in the south to the Black Forest and the Bavarian Alps. The Rhine River, which flows through much of Germany, is the most important waterway in Europe. Germany has many other rivers and canals that form a network of water highways.

Bordered by eight neighboring countries on all sides, Germany has few natural boundaries. Its geographical location in the heart of the European continent has made it a historical arena for invasions and wars.

Throughout its history, Germany has been a united country only twice, from 1871 to 1945 and since 1990. After its defeat in World War II in 1945, Germany became once again a divided country. West Germany, which had been occupied by England, France, and the United States after the war, became democratic, and East Germany, which had been occupied by the Soviet Union, became communist. Berlin, the former national capital, was also divided between East and West. In 1990, the two Germanys were once more united and became the Federal Republic of Germany, with Berlin as its official capital.

The German language **(Deutsch)** is spoken by 120 million people. It is the official language of Germany, Austria, and Liechtenstein and one of the four official languages of Switzerland. German is also the first language of 300,000 people in Luxembourg and the mother tongue of millions of people in other European countries, the United States, Canada, and South America.

Modern German is one of the Germanic languages derived from the old Indo-European family of languages spoken three thousand to four thousand years ago in Central Europe. The German people are the descendants of various Germanic tribes that settled in Central and Northern Europe at least two thousand years ago.

NOTE TO TEACHERS

➡ Have students learn more about Germany and German-speaking countries by doing research projects, either as written or oral reports.

- ◆ Topics for research may involve choosing a country, finding its size, population, capital city, bordering countries, language(s) spoken besides German, colors of the flag (see Note to Teachers, page 46), currency used, typical foods and dishes, holidays, dress, and so on. Prepare guiding questions to help focus students' attention on the topic chosen.

- ◆ Have students bring maps, photographs from travel brochures or magazines, authentic photographs taken by friends or relatives, souvenirs, and music.

- ◆ Have students create a display for the classroom.

Kulturwinkel (Supplementary Culture)

Many great German figures in science, philosophy, architecture, music, film, and art have contributed to the country's rich heritage. Below is a brief outline of the most influential German thinkers and writers. You may wish students to research the people listed or supplement the list with additional figures of importance or interest to the students.

➡ A few of the most important German scientists are:

- **Johannes Gutenberg** (1397–1468). Prior to Gutenberg's invention of the printing press, all reading material was laboriously written by hand, making the expensive and fragile books accessible only to a privileged few. The printing press was a historical breakthrough because it allowed greater dissemination of written materials. In 1455, Gutenberg printed the first version of the Latin Bible.

- **Nicolaus Copernicus** (1473–1543) and **Johannes Kepler** (1571–1630) shook the foundations of medieval thought by proposing that the Earth was not the center of the universe, but that it and the other planets moved around the sun.

- **Sigmund Freud** (1856–1939), a Viennese physician, set the stage for the development of psychology and psychiatry in the twentieth century. He was the founder of psychoanalysis.

- **Heinrich Hertz** (1857–1894) laid the foundations for the development of radio, television, and radar.

- **Max Planck** (1858–1947) discovered the quantum theory of energy, and **Albert Einstein** (1879–1955) strongly influenced the course of modern physics and our understanding of the universe. His theory of relativity created new concepts of space, time, mass, motion, and gravitation.

➡ The thought and philosophy of **Immanuel Kant, Arthur Schopenhauer, Georg Friedrich Hegel, Karl Marx,** and **Friedrich Nietzsche** had a marked influence on the work of major European philosophers, psychologists, novelists, and poets of the nineteenth and twentieth centuries.

➡ Many German writers have become world famous. Among them **Johann Wolfgang von Goethe** (*Faust*), **Thomas Mann** (*The Magic Mountain*), **Franz Kafka** (*The Trial*), **Erich Maria Remarque** (*All Quiet on the Western Front*).

➡ Many of the world's greatest composers come from Germany: **Johann Sebastian Bach, Ludwig van Beethoven, Johannes Brahms, Georg Friedrich Händel, Franz Josef Haydn, Wolfgang Amadeus Mozart, Franz Schubert, Robert Schumann, Johann** and **Richard Strauss, Richard Wagner.**

The first writing in German dates from the eighth century. One form of German, Low German, developed in the low, northern plains. Low German has many similarities to Dutch, Flemish, and English, which are also Germanic in origin. Another form, High German, developed in the higher, southern part of the country. High German became the standard German used today. Two of the most important developments in the history of the German language were Johannes Gutenberg's invention of movable type for printing in 1440 and Martin Luther's translation of the Bible into High German in the sixteenth century.

Many German-speaking people took their language with them when they went to live in other parts of the world. For example, Yiddish is based on German dialects spoken in the Middle Ages by Jews who emigrated to eastern Europe and is still spoken by many of their descendants throughout the world today.

Germany has become famous for the achievements of its scientists and engineers. Over the centuries, Germany has also produced many great poets, writers, philosophers, and composers, whose works have won renown throughout the world. The cultural richness of Germany extends into the everyday life of its people. Germans love and practice many sports and enjoy celebrations of all kinds. They like rich, delicious foods, many of which — like sausage and beer — have become worldwide staples.

Unlike English, French, and Spanish, the German language did not spread through colonization. Rather, many people have learned German in order to be able to read, study, and enjoy the works of the many great thinkers who have written in that language. Because of their common origin, German and English have many words that are similar — even identical — to each other. Only their pronunciation differs. These similarities will help you as you begin to learn German.

Kulturwinkel (Supplementary Culture)

Students may be interested in examples of foods and dishes of German-speaking countries.

➡ There are approximately 1,400 kinds of **Wurst** *(sausage)* in Germany. The most important kinds are **Leberwurst,** liverwurst; **Blutwurst,** blood sausage; **Bratwurst,** spicy pork sausage; **Mettwurst,** ground pork sausage. The German **Frankfurter** is thinner than the American variety and generally served in pairs. Sausages are not served on buns but are accompanied by a slice of bread or a roll.

➡ There are approximately two hundred kinds of bread and thirty kinds of rolls in the German-speaking world. The main types of German breads are **Weißbrot** (white bread), **Graubrot** (wheat and rye mixture), **Schwarzbrot** (rye bread), and **Pumpernickel** (heavy, dark bread).

➡ Sandwiches, usually made with sausage, ham or cheese, are generally open-faced with no bread on top and sometimes eaten with knife and fork.

➡ **Sauerkraut,** one of Germany's best-known foods, was developed to preserve cabbage and prevent it from spoiling.

ANSWERS TO ÜBUNG

1. *The Black Forest and the Bavarian Alps are located in the South.*

2. *The Rhine is the most important river and waterway in Europe.*

3. *In 1945, after its defeat in World War II, Germany was divided into West Germany, occupied by England, France, and the United States, which became democratic, and East Germany, occupied by the Soviet Union, which became communist.*

4. *Berlin*

5. *Germany, Austria, and Liechtenstein*

6. *Switzerland*

7. *Writing developed in the eighth century.*

8. *Dutch, Flemish, English, and German*

9. *It developed in the higher southern part of the country.*

10. *Johannes Gutenberg's invention of movable type for printing in 1440 and Martin Luther's translation of the Bible into High German in the sixteenth century*

11. *sausage and beer*

1. In which part of Germany are the Black Forest and the Bavarian Alps?

_____

2. What is the Rhine? _____

3. When and why was Germany divided into West Germany and East Germany?

_____

_____

4. What is the official capital of Germany? _____

5. In which three countries of Europe is German the only official language?

_____

6. In which European country is German one of four official languages?

_____

7. When did writing develop in Germany? _____

8. Name four Germanic languages. _____

_____

9. Why is the German from the southern part of Germany called High

German? _____

10. Which two events were important to the history of the German language?

_____

_____

11. Name two famous food products of Germany. _____

_____

2 German Cognates

You already know many German words. Some German words are spelled exactly like English words and have the same meanings: **Ball**, **Name**, **Hand**, **Sofa**, **warm**, **wild**. Many other German words are spelled almost like English words, differing only in one or two letters: **Amerika**, **Fisch**, **Kaffee**, **Prinz**. In these words and many others, English hard *c* becomes German **k**, English *sh* becomes German **sch**, and English soft *c* becomes German **z**. Some other German cognates have two dots — called Umlaut — over the vowels **a**, **o**, and **u**. This Umlaut changes the pronunciation of the vowel: **Bäcker** = *baker*, **Öl** = *oil*, **grün** = *green*.

How many of the following German words can you understand? Fill the blanks with their English meanings. If you need to, you may look in a dictionary:

1. Amerika _____

2. Appetit _____

3. Armee _____

4. Asche _____

5. Bäcker _____

6. Banane _____

7. blond _____

8. braun _____

9. Busch _____

10. Diamant _____

11. Eisberg _____

12. elegant _____

13. Ende _____

14. Energie _____

15. Familie _____

16. Fingernagel _____

17. Fisch _____

18. Garten _____

19. Gras _____

20. Haar _____

➡ Cognates provide a perfect opportunity to delight students with early discovery of words they can easily associate with what they already know.

➡ Point out to students that 25 percent of English words come from German, the language of the Angles and Saxons, Germanic tribes who invaded Britain beginning about the year 450. The Anglo-Saxons ruled until 1066, when they were defeated by an invading army from France. For the next two centuries, French was England's official language, but the common people continued to use Anglo-Saxon. The basic words of English today are of Anglo-Saxon origin: articles, the words for numbers, many prepositions and conjunctions, pronouns, and many commonly used verbs and nouns.

ANSWERS TO ÜBUNG

1. *America*	11. *iceberg*
2. *appetite*	12. *elegant*
3. *army*	13. *end*
4. *ash*	14. *energy*
5. *baker*	15. *family*
6. *banana*	16. *fingernail*
7. *blond*	17. *fish*
8. *brown*	18. *garden*
9. *bush*	19. *grass*
10. *diamond*	20. *hair*

ANSWERS TO ÜBUNG

21. *house*
22. *hundred*
23. *engineer*
24. *insect*
25. *January*
26. *July*
27. *June*
28. *young*
29. *coffee*
30. *class*
31. *concert*
32. *corn*
33. *crocodile*
34. *lamp*
35. *loud*
36. *lip*
37. *May*
38. *man*
39. *machine*
40. *mathematics*
41. *mouse*
42. *milk*
43. *music*

44. *number*
45. *officer*
46. *police*
47. *prince*
48. *round*
49. *shoe*
50. *Spanish*

NOTE TO TEACHERS

You may want students to look at the advertisements on page 9 and guess the meanings of the German words that have English cognates.

21. Haus _____

22. hundert _____

23. Ingenieur _____

24. Insekt _____

25. Januar _____

26. Juli _____

27. Juni _____

28. jung _____

29. Kaffee _____

30. Klasse _____

31. Konzert _____

32. Korn _____

33. Krokodil _____

34. Lampe _____

35. laut _____

36. Lippe _____

37. Mai _____

38. Mann _____

39. Maschine _____

40. Mathematik _____

41. Maus _____

42. Milch _____

43. Musik _____

44. Nummer _____

45. Offizier _____

46. Polizei _____

47. Prinz _____

48. rund _____

49. Schuh _____

50. Spanisch _____

SOMMER IN AMERIKA
Juli – August
NONSTOPFLUG
FRANKFURT
NEW YORK
LOS ANGELES

DER DIAMANT IM GRAS

DAS KORN IST GRÜN

ST-PAULUS-KIRCHE

KONZERT
BACH VIVALDI MOZART

Café Heidelberg
Kennedyallee 45
Das Restaurant
für die Familie

3 German Names

Now that you are able to recognize over 50 German words resembling English, let's look at how German and English names compare.

Udo is going to help you learn how to pronounce some of these names.

You will meet **Udo** throughout this book holding his lens over one or two pronunciation clues he wants to share with you as you develop a good German pronunciation.

Whenever you look at **Udo's** clues, keep this in mind: every time you try to pronounce a German sound, hold your mouth, tongue, lips, and teeth in the same position at the end of the sound as you did at the beginning. Try saying **o** this way. Now try **oooo**. Again, try saying **u** this way. Now try **uuuu**. There, you've got it.

Udo has two clues for you before you listen to the following list of boys' and girls' names. The first one tells you how to pronounce HIS name:

The second clue tells you how to pronounce the German **r**.

Bruno

braun, rund

NOTE TO TEACHERS

➡ In each section, students encounter **Udo,** who will teach them pronunciation skills. Emphasize the phonetic concepts **Udo** presents. Model all German words for students and/or have them listen to the cassette. Have students repeat individually and in unison.

➡ To teach and practice the German sounds **Udo** presents in the book, you may wish to illustrate on cards two or three words containing the sounds introduced. Use the cards throughout the course to review sounds already studied.

➡ To have more fun with **Udo** and his clues, bring an oversized jacket and hat to class. Have students play **Udo,** wearing the jacket and hat as they model the sounds and words of **Udo's** clues to the class.

➡ Children love to say the alphabet. Have students learn and practice the German alphabet at a point in the course where they have attained some familiarity with German sounds and spellings, especially the long and short vowels. You may reproduce the alphabet for students and have the class repeat it several times, gaining speed with each repetition. You may also have students sing a familiar alphabet tune from nursery school, this time in German.

Alphabet

Letter	Name	Sound	Example
a	ah	*a* in *father*	**Tag** (*day*)
ä	ah Umlaut	*ai* in *fair*	**Bäcker** (*baker*)
b	beh	*b* in *boy*	**Bett** (*bed*)
c	tseh	*c* in *cat*	**Café** (*café*)
d	deh	*d* in *day*	**danke** (*thank you*)
e	eh	*e* in *they*	**Tee** (*tea*)
f	eff	*f* in *foot*	**Fuß** (*foot*)
g	geh	*g* in *go*	**gut** (*good*)
h	hah	*h* in *hand*	**Hand** (*hand*)
i	ih	*i* in *machine*	**sie** (*she*)
		i in *fish*	**Fisch** (*fish*)
j	jot	*y* in *yes*	**ja** (*yes*)
k	kah	*k* in *king*	**Kugelschreiber** (*pen*)
l	ell	*l* in *live*	**Lehrer** (*teacher*)
m	emm	*m* in *me*	**Maus** (*mouse*)
n	enn	*n* in *no*	**nein** (*no*)
o	oh	*o* in *open*	**Ohr** (*ear*)

Alphabet (continued)

Letter	Name	Sound	Example
ö	oh Umlaut	Round lips for *o* in *come* and pronounce *e* in *they*.	**zwölf** (*twelve*)
p	peh	*p* in *post*	**Papier** (*paper*)
q	kuh	pronounced *kv*	**Qualität** (*quality*)
r	err	almost like a gargle	**rot** (*red*)
s	ess	*s* in *this* *z* in *zoo* *sh* in *shut* before *t* or *p*	**Glas** (*glass*) **sieben** (*seven*) **Stuhl** (*chair*)
ß	ess-tsett	*s* in *house*	**Fuß** (*foot*)
t	teh	*t* in *table*	**Tisch** (*table*)
u	uh	*oo* in *moon*	**Junge** (*boy*)
ü	uh Umlaut	Round lips for *oo* in *moon* and pronounce *i* in *machine*.	**Tür** (*door*)
v	fau	*f* in *four*	**vier** (*four*)
w	veh	*v* in *valve*	**was** (*what*)
x	iks	*ks* in *books*	**Taxi** (*taxi*)
y	üpsilon	like **ü** above	**Mythe** (*myth*)
z	tsett	*ts* in *cats*	**zehn** (*ten*)
ai	aï	*i* in *night*	**Mai** (*May*)
au	au	*ou* in *ouch*	**Haus** (*house*)
äu	oi	*oy* in *toy*	**Gebäude** (*building*)
ei	aï	*i* in *night*	**nein** (*no*)
eu	oi	*oy* in *toy*	**heute** (*today*)

NOTE TO TEACHERS

➡ Have each student choose a German name.

➡ As students practice vowel sounds, explain that German vowels may be long or short. Practice with contrasting long and short vowels. Stress that it is important to make short vowels really short:

LONG: Klara   Erika   Udo   Bruno
SHORT: Hans   Jens   Lotte   Kurt

➡ Have students make name tags for the German names they have chosen. Students may write **Ich heiße** before their German names.

Here is a list of boys' and girls' names. With your teacher's help, choose a German name that you would like to have for yourself while you are studying German:

Alois	Hans	Herbert	Jürgen	Konrad
Anton	Heinz	Jens	Karl	Kurt
Augustin	Helmut	Johann	Klaus	Lars
Bernd				Leopold
Boris				Ludwig
Bruno				Michael
Christian				Oskar
Daniel				Otto
Dieter				Richard
Dirk				Rudi
Edgar				Thomas
Emil				Udo
Fritz				Viktor
Günther				Wolfgang

Agnes	Ilse	Jutta	Lotte	Margot
Andrea	Inge	Karin	Luise	Maria
Annemarie	Ingrid	Klara	Magda	Marianne
Brigitte				Marlene
Christine				Monika
Claudia				Olga
Erika				Petra
Gisela				Renate
Gretel				Sabine
Heidi				Silke
Heike				Stefanie
Helga				Susanne
Hilde				Ulrike

When Germans want to say, "My name is Heinrich," they say, **"Ich heiße Heinrich."** Practice telling your teacher and your classmates your name in German. If you and your teacher have chosen German names, use them.

Udo's clue:

Hans, Karin

NOTE TO TEACHERS

➡ This **Übung** gives students immediate experience in using the language. If students have made German name tags, use them.

- ◆ Point to yourself and, **"Ich heiße** _____ (your name)."**
- ◆ Then point to a student and ask, **"Wie heißt du?"** If the student does not understand, repeat your name. Model **"Ich heiße"** again until the student catches on.

Repeat these two phrases with several students, giving as many as possible a chance both to ask and answer the question.

You can find the English equivalents of all German phrases in the end Vocabulary. All German materials are included in the cassette program.

➡ At this point, explain that the letter combination **ß**, pronounced *s*, may be replaced by **ss** when writing.

➡ *Udo's clue:* Model pronunciation of the German **a** sound for students. You may wish to refer students to the list of names on page 11 to find and pronounce additional words containing this sound.

NOTE TO TEACHERS

➡ Before students are asked to read Dialog 1 for meaning, have them look at the characters and guess what Hans and Karin may be saying to each other in each illustration.

➡ Next, model pronunciation either by reading aloud or by playing the cassette while students read the dialog.

➡ Have students close their books. Read short segments for students to repeat. If a phrase is too long, break it into shorter sections, reading the last part first. Have students repeat, then add another word or two until you have read the entire segment. Have students repeat after each addition. For example:

Und du?
Karin. Und du?
Ich heiße Karin. Und du?

➡ Ask questions:

  ◆ How do the boy and girl say hello?

  ◆ What does the girl ask the boy?

  ◆ What is the boy's name?

  ◆ Are they happy to meet each other?

  ◆ What do they say to each other?

  ◆ How do they say good-bye?

➡ Note that the optional dialog, Dialog 4, **"Guten Abend,"** introducing **Sie,** is included on page 55 of the Teacher Annotations. You may reproduce it for your students if you wish to teach the **Sie** form. Introduce Dialog 4 at the end of Section 10, "Talking About Yourself."

* **du** means you in German; **du** is used when you are speaking to a close relative, a friend, or a child — someone with whom you are familiar. To say *you*, the Germans also use **Sie** when speaking to a stranger or a grown-up — a person with whom you should be formal. The exercises in this book use **du**.

Now let's review what you learned in Dialog 1:

1. Guten Tag, _____ (name).

Guten Tag, _____ (name).

2. Wie heißt du?

Ich heiße _____. Und du? Wie heißt du?

3. Freut mich, _____ (name).

Freut mich auch, _____ (name).

4. Auf Wiedersehen!

Auf Wiedersehen!

Note to Teachers

➡ Introduce the words **Herr, Frau, Fräulein** on the chalkboard by writing the words before names of people students know. Model pronunciation for the class.

➡ Greet students and ask them to respond by greeting you with **"Guten Tag, Frau (Fräulein, Herr) _____."** Have students take turns greeting each other.

➡ Tell students your name, then ask theirs. Have students ask their classmates their names.

➡ Circulate among students, shaking hands with them as you say, **"Freut mich"**; and they reply, **"Freut mich auch."**

➡ In pairs, have students practice the vocabulary of Dialog 1. Challenge students to improvise a skit in front of the class between two people who have just met, ending with **"Auf Wiedersehen, Frau (Fräulein, Herr) _____."**

➡ Explain to students that in German, if you know the name of the person you address, it is considered impolite not to use it.

Kulturwinkel (Supplementary Culture)

You may wish to explain the following points on German greetings.

- ◆ People in a rush sometimes abbreviate their greeting and say **"Morgen!"** instead of **"Guten Morgen."**

- ◆ Our English *Hello* and *Hi* have almost become international greetings, and most Germans will use them when greeting Americans. Children have also started using *Hello* to greet other children and at times adults.

- ◆ When Germans are introduced to each other, they shake hands, smile, and nod their head. The Germans do not use the English polite greeting, *How do you do?* In Germany, this greeting is reserved for someone you know and from whom you expect a lengthy, detailed answer.

- ◆ When greeting someone you know with a handshake, it is usually the woman or the older person who offers the hand first. When meeting in the street or in public places, people shake hands only if they intend to stop and chat for a while. If they are just passing by, men remove their hat or make a gesture as if about to remove it while saying **"Guten Tag!"** When two couples greet each other at the same time, care must be taken not to shake hands crosswise since this is believed to bring bad luck. To avoid this predicament, the women shake hands first.

- ◆ There is no German equivalent of English *Ms.* The German solution to *Ms.* is to call both married and unmarried women **Frau. Fräulein** is used only for very young, unmarried girls.

Greetings!

Germans customarily shake hands more frequently than Americans when they greet each other. People usually shake hands every time they meet and every time they part. Except for close relatives, it is not common in Germany to kiss women on the cheek. But it is still customary in Germany for a man to remove his hat or cap when greeting a woman.

Here are some common German greetings:

Tag!	Hi!, Hello! (informal)
Guten Tag!	Hello!, Good day! (formal)
Guten Morgen!	Good morning!
Guten Abend!	Good evening!
Gute Nacht!	Good night!
(Auf) Wiedersehen!	Good-bye!
Tschüs!	Bye-bye!, So long!

4 Numbers

Udo's clues:

e = eh

i = ee of meet

zehn, s**ie**ben

You will soon be able to count to forty in German. Listen to your teacher or the cassette to learn how to say the numbers 1 to 20.

1 eins
2 zwei
3 drei
4 vier
5 fünf
6 sechs
7 sieben
8 acht
9 neun
10 zehn
11 elf
12 zwölf
13 dreizehn
14 vierzehn
15 fünfzehn
16 sechzehn
17 siebzehn
18 achtzehn
19 neunzehn
20 zwanzig

➡ *Udo's clues:* Model pronunciation of the German **e** and **i** sounds for students. For additional practice words, refer to the list of cognates on pages 8 and 9, or the list of names on page 11.

➡ Model pronunciation of numbers 1 to 10 or have students listen to the cassette, allowing time for repetition.

➡ Have students repeat groups of numbers:

- ◆ **eins, zwei, drei / vier, fünf, sechs / sieben, acht, neun, zehn**
- ◆ **eins, zwei, drei, vier, fünf / sechs, sieben, acht, neun, zehn**
- ◆ **zehn, neun, acht, sieben, sechs, fünf, vier, drei, zwei, eins**
- ◆ **zwei, vier, sechs, acht, zehn / eins, drei, fünf, sieben, neun**

➡ **Wie viele?** = *How many?* Hold up one finger, then two, then three, and so on. Each time, ask, **"Wie viele?"** allowing the whole class time to respond.

➡ Model pronunciation of numbers 11 to 20 or have students listen to the cassette, allowing time for repetition.

➡ Have students repeat these numbers in groups, as above.

➡ Count from **eins** to **zwanzig** with even numbers, then with odd.

➡ As a listening comprehension activity, have each student write his or her telephone number, real or made up, on a piece of paper. Students then drop the telephone numbers into a box. Choose a student to pick a number from the box and read it aloud in German to the class. As soon as the telephone number is recognized, the student yells out, **"Das ist meine!"** *(It's mine!).* That student then picks another number from the box and reads it aloud to the class.

➡ Indicate people and objects in the classroom: the teacher, light(s), desk, books on the desk, doors, windows, pencils, girls, boys. After pointing to a person or object or to a group of people or objects, query, **"Wie viele?"**

➡ As a vocabulary study aid for students, you may wish to duplicate the format of this first **Übung** in each of the following sections. List German words to be learned in the left column followed by blank rules. List English equivalents in the right column. Illustrations may substitute for English equivalents.

➡ Have students write the numbers they hear, stopping after every four numbers to check answers.

ANSWERS TO ÜBUNG (teacher dictation in brackets)

1. [dreizehn] **13**	**5.** [eins] **1**	**9.** [zwölf] **12**
2. [vier] **4**	**6.** [achtzehn] **18**	**10.** [elf] **11**
3. [neunzehn] **19**	**7.** [fünf] **5**	**11.** [sechzehn] **16**
4. [siebzehn] **17**	**8.** [fünfzehn] **15**	**12.** [zwanzig] **20**

➡ Here is a song to practice numbers. Assign each student a number from 1 to 20. Instruct students to strike a pose and freeze when they hear their number. Students are free to move only when their number is sung again. You may wish to adapt this song to practice numbers 21 to 40.

Eins, zwei, drei

1. Eins zwei drei vier fünf sechs sie-ben acht Eins zwei drei vier fünf sechs sie-ben acht,

Eins zwei drei vier fünf sechs sie-ben acht Neun zehn elf zwölf drei - zehn.

2. Vierzehn, fünfzehn, sechszehn, siebzehn Mark. Vierzehn, fünfzehn, sechszehn, siebzehn Mark,
Vierzehn, fünfzehn, sechszehn, siebzehn Mark. Achtzehn, neunzehn, zwanzig.

© 1994, Uwe Kind

Translation   ONE, TWO, THREE
1. *One, two, three, four, five, six, seven, eight,*   2. *Fourteen, fifteen, sixteen, seventeen Marks,*
One, two, three, four, five, six, seven, eight.   *Fourteen, fifteen, sixteen, seventeen Marks.*
One, two, three, four, five, six, seven, eight,   *Fourteen, fifteen, sixteen, seventeen Marks,*
Nine, ten, eleven, twelve, thirteen.   *Eighteen, nineteen, twenty.*

1. Cover page 16 with a sheet of paper. Then cover the German number words below and say the numbers aloud in German.

2. Now cover the German number words and write the German number words in the blank lines.

siebzehn	_____	17	fünfzehn	_____	15
acht	_____	8	sechzehn	_____	16
drei	_____	3	sieben	_____	7
eins	_____	1	vier	_____	4
neun	_____	9	achtzehn	_____	18
elf	_____	11	zwölf	_____	12
dreizehn	_____	13	vierzehn	_____	14
fünf	_____	5	zehn	_____	10
neunzehn	_____	19	zwanzig	_____	20
sechs	_____	6	zwei	_____	2

3. Pretend you are the teacher and correct your work with a red pen or pencil. You will be able to see at a glance which words you need to study further.

ÜBUNG

Your teacher will read some German numbers to you. Write the numerals for the number you hear:

1._____   4._____   7._____   10._____

2._____   5._____   8._____   11._____

3._____   6._____   9._____   12._____

Let's continue learning numbers. Listen to your teacher or the cassette to learn how to say the numbers 21 to 40.

ÜBUNG

Cover the top of page 18 with a sheet of paper while you do the next three activities. Your teacher will read some numbers from 21 to 40 in random order to you. Write the numerals for the German number you hear:

1. _____   6. _____

2. _____   7. _____

3. _____   8. _____

4. _____   9. _____

5. _____   10. _____

NOTE TO TEACHERS

➡ Model pronunciation of numbers 21 to 30 or have students listen to the cassette, allowing time for repetition.

➡ Ask students if they see a pattern in the numbers 21 to 30. After they point out the pattern, ask them to try to compose the numbers 31 to 39 aloud.

➡ Now model pronunciation of numbers 31 to 40 or have students listen to the cassette, allowing time for repetition.

➡ Have students repeat groups of numbers sequentially, even and odd, forward and then backward.

➡ Have students repeat numbers 20 to 40 in multiples of 2 and 5, forward and then backward.

➡ For additional review, write a German number word on a piece of paper for each student in the class. Distribute numbers at random. Have students line up in the correct number order. Once lined up, have students yell out their numbers in sequence.

➡ For authentic practice in writing number words, distribute copies of blank checks with a dollar amount from 1 to 40 written in digits. Have students complete the checks by writing the dollar amount in words.

➡ Have students write the numbers they hear, stopping after every five numbers to check answers.

ANSWERS TO ÜBUNG *(teacher dictation in brackets)*

1. [zwanzig] **20**
2. [vierzig] **40**
3. [dreißig] **30**
4. [einundzwanzig] **21**
5. [einunddreißig] **31**

6. [dreiunddreißig] **33**
7. [vierundzwanzig] **24**
8. [achtundzwanzig] **28**
9. [sechsunddreißig] **36**
10. [siebenundzwanzig] **27**

ANSWERS TO ÜBUNG

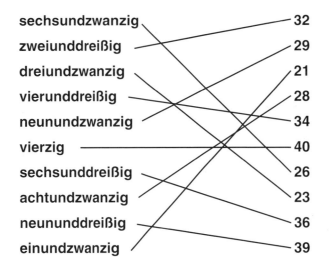

sechsundzwanzig — 32
zweiunddreißig — 29
dreiundzwanzig — 21
vierunddreißig — 28
neunundzwanzig — 34
vierzig — 40
sechsunddreißig — 26
achtundzwanzig — 23
neununddreißig — 36
einundzwanzig — 39

Have students write the German number words for the numbers they hear, stopping after every five numbers to check answers.

ANSWERS TO ÜBUNG *(teacher dictation in brackets)*

1. [thirty-two] *zweiunddreißig*
2. [twenty-three] *dreiundzwanzig*
3. [thirty-seven] *siebenunddreißig*
4. [twenty-nine] *neunundzwanzig*
5. [twenty-six] *sechsundzwanzig*
6. [thirty-four] *vierunddreißig*
7. [thirty-eight] *achtunddreißig*
8. [twenty-two] *zweiundzwanzig*
9. [thirty-nine] *neununddreißig*
10. [twenty-five] *fünfundzwanzig*

See how many German number words you can recognize. Draw a line to match the German number word with its numeral:

sechsundzwanzig	32
zweiunddreißig	29
dreiundzwanzig	21
vierunddreißig	28
neunundzwanzig	34
vierzig	40
sechsunddreißig	26
achtundzwanzig	23
neununddreißig	36
einundzwanzig	39

Now your teacher will read some numbers in English. Write the number words in German:

1. _____   6. _____

2. _____   7. _____

3. _____   8. _____

4. _____   9. _____

5. _____   10. _____

Now that you know the numbers from 1 to 40, let's try some math. First let's look at some words you will need to know:

Now write the answers to the following arithmetic problems in German. Then find the correct answers in the puzzle. Circle them from left to right, right to left, up or down, or diagonally:

1. zehn weniger sechs ist _____

2. achtzehn und sechs ist _____

3. dreizehn weniger drei ist _____

4. zehn und zehn ist _____

5. acht und sechs ist _____

6. eins und sieben ist _____

7. fünfzehn weniger zwei ist _____

8. acht und acht ist _____

9. zehn und zwei ist _____

10. zwölf und sechs ist _____

11. vierzig weniger achtunddreißig ist _____

12. sieben weniger vier ist _____

NOTE TO TEACHERS

➡ Explain arithmetical expressions to students:

- ◆ **und** = *and, plus*
- ◆ **weniger** = *minus, less*
- ◆ **ist** = *is, equals*

➡ You may wish to adapt the number song on page 17 to practice numbers 21 to 40.

➡ Indicate to students that for this and all subsequent word searches and puzzles, umlauts are not included.

ANSWERS TO ÜBUNG

1. *vier*

2. *vierundzwanzig*

3. *zehn*

4. *zwanzig*

5. *vierzehn*

6. *acht*

7. *dreizehn*

8. *sechzehn*

9. *zwölf*

10. *achtzehn*

11. *zwei*

12. *drei*

13. *fünf*

14. *elf*

15. *sieben*

16. *fünfzehn*

17. *siebzehn*

18. *neunzehn*

19. *neun*

20. *neunundzwanzig*

13. fünfzehn weniger zehn ist _____

14. dreißig weniger neunzehn ist _____

15. sechzehn weniger neun ist _____

16. dreizehn und zwei ist _____

17. neun und acht ist _____

18. zwanzig weniger eins ist _____

19. sechs und drei ist _____

20. vierzig weniger elf ist _____

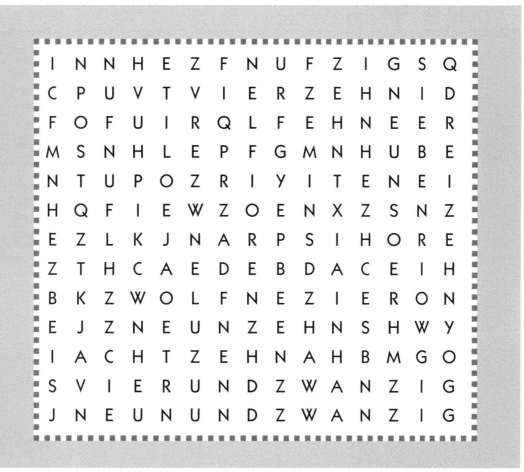

I	N	N	H	E	Z	F	N	U	F	Z	I	G	S	Q
C	P	U	V	T	V	I	E	R	Z	E	H	N	I	D
F	O	F	U	I	R	Q	L	F	E	H	N	E	E	R
M	S	N	H	L	E	P	F	G	M	N	H	U	B	E
N	T	U	P	O	Z	R	I	Y	I	T	E	N	E	I
H	Q	F	I	E	W	Z	O	E	N	X	Z	S	N	Z
E	Z	L	K	J	N	A	R	P	S	I	H	O	R	E
Z	T	H	C	A	E	D	E	B	D	A	C	E	I	H
B	K	Z	W	O	L	F	N	E	Z	I	E	R	O	N
E	J	Z	N	E	U	N	Z	E	H	N	S	H	W	Y
I	A	C	H	T	Z	E	H	N	A	H	B	M	G	O
S	V	I	E	R	U	N	D	Z	W	A	N	Z	I	G
J	N	E	U	N	U	N	D	Z	W	A	N	Z	I	G

5 Days of the Week

Udo's clue:

Vowels with Umlaut do not exist in English.

- Pronounce **ä** like *e* in *bed.*
- For **ö**, round your lips for *o* in *rope* and pronounce *e* in *they.*
- For **ü**, round your lips as if about to whistle and pronounce *ee* in *meet.*

März, Öl, fünf

MONTAG	DIENSTAG	MITTWOCH	DONNERSTAG	FREITAG	SAMSTAG	SONNTAG
1	2	3	4	5	6	7
8	9	10	11	12	13	14
15	16	17	18	19	20	21
22	23	24	25	26	27	28
29	30	31				

NOVEMBER

These are the days of the week in German. The German week begins with Monday.

Heute ist Montag. = *Today is Monday.*

Each day, find as many people as you can and tell them the day of the week in German.

➡ *Udo's clue:* Model pronunciation of German vowels with umlauts, **ä, ö,** and **ü,** for students.

➡ After drilling the days of the week with a wall calendar or calendar transparency, have students take turns greeting the class with, **"Guten Tag! Heute ist _____."**

➡ At the beginning of each class period, have a different student greet the class, say the day of the week, and write it on the chalkboard.

➡ Here is a fun song to practice the days of the week. After the first verse, substitute the food and the day of the week as indicated in numbers three to seven.

Nudeltag

1. Was ist heut' für ein Tag? Heu-te ist Nu-del-tag.
Nu-del-tag ist im-mer Mon-tag. Mon-tag ist Nu-del-tag.

2. Was ist heut' für ein Tag? Heute ist Suppentag.
   Suppentag ist immer Dienstag. Dienstag ist Suppentag.

3. Sandwichtag   /   Mittwoch
4. Brezeltag   /   Donnerstag
5. Pizzatag   /   Freitag
6. Würstchentag   /   Samstag
7. Eiskremtag   /   Sonntag

© 1994, Uwe Kind

Translation   NOODLE DAY

1. *What kind of a day is today?*   3. *Sandwich day   /   Wednesday*
   Today is noodle day.
   Noodle day is always Monday.   4. *Pretzel day   /   Thursday*
   Monday is noodle day.
2. *What kind of a day is today?*   5. *Pizza day   /   Friday*
   Today is soup day.
   Soup day is always Tuesday.   6. *Sausage day   /   Saturday*
   Tuesday is soup day.
                                           7. *Ice cream day   /   Sunday*

➡ Students may be interested in comparing German and American school systems and school life.

    ◆ German children are required by law to attend school from age six to fifteen. As in the United States, the organization of the school system is the responsibility of the states.

    ◆ Though not mandatory, many children attend **Kindergarten** before they begin first grade.

    ◆ After finishing four years of elementary school, students attend one of three types of secondary schools:

      1. The **Hauptschule** prepares students for a trade. After five years of formal education, **Hauptschule** graduates can continue on to the **Berufschule,** *trade school,* or go on to a hands-on apprenticeship under a skilled craftsperson in their field.

      2. The **Realschule** prepares students for more highly skilled positions. After six years of studies, graduates from the **Realschule** may go on to further their education in a **Fachschule,** *technical college.*

      3. The **Gymnasium,** *academic high school,* prepares students to continue their education in the university. Students must pass a special test at the end of nine years of studies at the **Gymnasium** in order to qualify for university admission.

➡ German schools are strictly for learning and play no role in the student's social life, other than the occasional day trips and annual excursion. Although schools do have a physical education program, extra-curricular activities like sports, commencement ceremonies, honor societies, clubs, dances, school rings, or yearbooks are unknown in German schools.

➡ Schools in Germany generally do not meet as long each day as American schools. Students have no lunch hour at school, but go home around one o'clock. However, classes are held six days a week.

➡ The relationship between teachers and students is much more formal than in the United States. The casual, friendly atmosphere that one often finds in an American school classroom is almost unknown in Germany. In the classroom, the teacher is treated with deference and respect. Students rise when the teacher enters the classroom.

Kulturwinkel **In der Schule** (At school)

Complete the following school schedule with the subjects you are taking this year:

	MONTAG	DIENSTAG	MITTWOCH	DONNERSTAG	FREITAG

Now look at a typical schedule of a German student. Compare it with yours. What are the differences? What are the similarities?

	MONTAG	DIENSTAG	MITTWOCH	DONNERSTAG	FREITAG	SAMSTAG
8.00 – 8.45	Math	German	English	Math	German	Religion
8.45 – 9.30	History	Biology	English	German	Biology	History
9.30 – 10.15	English	Art	History	Social Studies	Math	Geography
10.40 – 11.25	Social Studies	Music	Religion	Latin	English	
11.25 – 12.10	Sports	Latin	Art	Geography	Needlework	
12.20 – 13.05	Sports	Needlework	Sports	Music	Sports	

There are usually short pauses between classes, and students normally stay in the same room for most classes. A longer recess (**Große Pause**) from 10:15 to 10:40 provides time for socializing and a mid-morning snack. The short recess (**Kleine Pause**) from 12:10 to 12:20 gives students some additional free time.

Parents of German students receive periodic report cards. Grades range from 1 to 6. Most students want an **"Eins"** (1), the highest grade. A grade of 5 or 6 is unsatisfactory.

What other differences can you see between American and German school days?

6 Months of the Year

The months of the year in German resemble English.
Can you recognize all of them?

JANUAR   FEBRUAR   MÄRZ   APRIL

MAI   JUNI   JULI   AUGUST

SEPTEMBER   OKTOBER   NOVEMBER   DEZEMBER

➡ You may wish to use a wall calendar or transparency to introduce the names of the months.

Drill the months by going up and down the rows, eliciting the names of the months sequentially **Januar** to **Dezember** and then backward **Dezember** to **Januar.** As students gain confidence, pick up speed.

➡ To practice the months of the year, students may enjoy saying a German version of the familiar "Thirty Days Has November."

DIE ZWÖLF MONATE

Dreißig Tage im November, April, Juni, September.
Achtundzwanzig ein einziger.
Die anderen einunddreißig.

Translation

THE 12 MONTHS

Thirty days has November, April, June, and September.
Of twenty-eight there's only one.
All the rest have thirty-one.

ANSWERS TO ÜBUNG

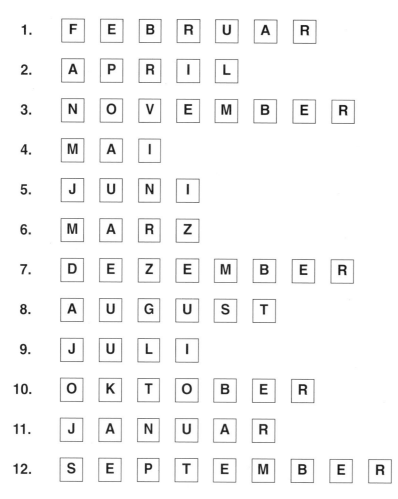

1. F E B R U A R
2. A P R I L
3. N O V E M B E R
4. M A I
5. J U N I
6. M A R Z
7. D E Z E M B E R
8. A U G U S T
9. J U L I
10. O K T O B E R
11. J A N U A R
12. S E P T E M B E R

Unscramble the letters to form the name of a German month:

1. B R E A F U R

2. P R A I L

3. B R E E N V O M

4. A I M

5. N U J I

6. Z R A M

7. B E Z E D R E M

8. S U G A T U

9. U J I L

10. T O B K E R O

11. N A U R A J

12. T E S M P R E B E

Match the names of the months with their numbers by drawing lines between the two columns. For example, January is number one and December is number twelve:

März	sieben
September	fünf
Juli	drei
Januar	vier
Dezember	zehn
August	zwei
April	neun
Oktober	zwölf
Februar	sechs
Mai	eins
November	acht
Juni	elf

ANSWERS TO ÜBUNG

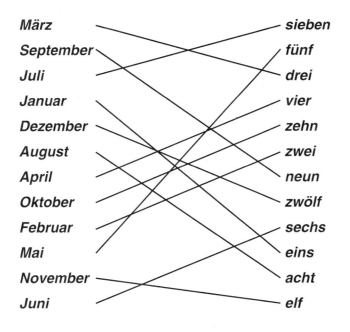

März	sieben
September	fünf
Juli	drei
Januar	vier
Dezember	zehn
August	zwei
April	neun
Oktober	zwölf
Februar	sechs
Mai	eins
November	acht
Juni	elf

Answers to Übung will vary.

NOTE TO TEACHERS

➡ Here is a song the class will enjoy to practice the months of the year. Have the students hold hands and walk in a circle as they sing. After the first verse, everyone stops, the children whose birthday is in January step inside the circle and act out the instructions of the song. Repeat the verses with other months of the year.

Wer im Januar Geburtstag hat . . .

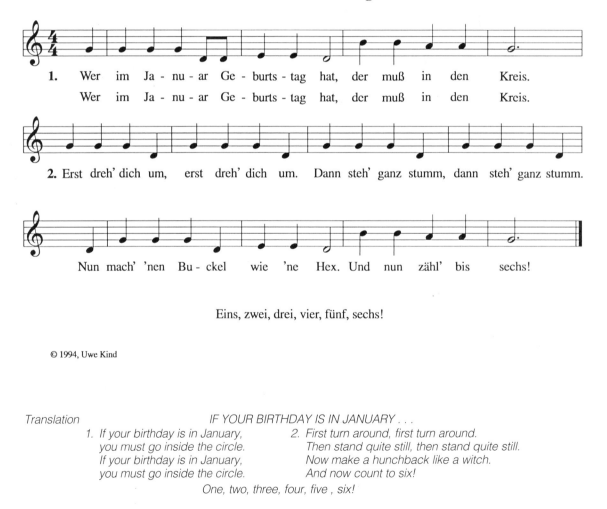

1. Wer im Ja - nu - ar Ge - burts - tag hat, der muß in den Kreis.
Wer im Ja - nu - ar Ge - burts - tag hat, der muß in den Kreis.

2. Erst dreh' dich um, erst dreh' dich um. Dann steh' ganz stumm, dann steh' ganz stumm.

Nun mach' 'nen Bu - ckel wie 'ne Hex. Und nun zähl' bis sechs!

Eins, zwei, drei, vier, fünf, sechs!

© 1994, Uwe Kind

Translation   IF YOUR BIRTHDAY IS IN JANUARY . . .

1. *If your birthday is in January,*   2. *First turn around, first turn around.*
   you must go inside the circle.   *Then stand quite still, then stand quite still.*
   If your birthday is in January,   *Now make a hunchback like a witch.*
   you must go inside the circle.   *And now count to six!*

One, two, three, four, five , six!

27   *Teacher Annotations*

Answer the following questions with the German months:

1. Which is your favorite month?

_____

2. Which is your least favorite month?

_____

3. In which month is your birthday?

_____

4. In which month does your mother celebrate her birthday?

_____

5. In which month does your father celebrate his birthday?

_____

6. In which month does your best friend celebrate her/his

birthday? _____

7. When does your teacher celebrate her/his birthday?

_____

8. In which months do you have vacation?

_____

Fill in the blanks with the correct German names of the days or months, then find the nineteen days or months in the puzzle. Circle them from left to right, right to left, up or down, or diagonally:

1. The day after Monday: _____

2. The day before Thursday: _____

3. The first day of the weekend: _____

4. Garfield hates this day: _____

5. Many people go to church
on this day of the week: _____

6. The day before Friday: _____

7. The last day of your school week: _____

8. The first month of the year: _____

9. The month of Christmas: _____

10. The month of Thanksgiving: _____

11. The month you go back to
school after the summer break: _____

12. Halloween is on the last day
of this month: _____

13. The month of the
United States' birthday: _____

14. Memorial Day occurs toward
the end of this month: _____

15. The month of St. Patrick's day: _____

ANSWERS TO ÜBUNG

1. *Dienstag*

2. *Mittwoch*

3. *Samstag*

4. *Montag*

5. *Sonntag*

6. *Donnerstag*

7. *Freitag*

8. *Januar*

9. *Dezember*

10. *November*

11. *September*

12. *Oktober*

13. *Juli*

14. *Mai*

15. *März*

ANSWERS TO ÜBUNG

16. *Juni*

17. *Februar*

18. *August*

19. *April*

16. Flag Day is celebrated in
this month: _____

17. The month of Valentine's Day: _____

18. The month after July: _____

19. April Fool's Day is the first day
of this month: _____

```
O K T O B E R A C T S U G U A
S D M U J U N I A S U V P Q R
T I G R O A P R I L O N U E N
D E G L E P N A G A T S M A S
O N T A Q B P U C P B A Q L O
N S G O T O M N A M E H E B N
N T L U J S I E P R L C F G N
E A N A H W N S Z E Z O D N T
R G J U L I X E L E M W R N A
S J J K H G F U I V D T L O G
T F E B R U A R H O I T B S E
A D I Z E N B R F R E I T A G
G I Q I G A T N O M O M A R Z
A R E B M E V O N A A D T S A
S E P T E M B E R I C O L P W
```

Now that you have learned the names of the days and months, let's learn how to say dates. When the Germans want to say, "Today is Monday, July fourteenth," they say, **"Heute ist Montag, der vierzehnte Juli."** "Today is Friday, March first" would be **"Heute ist Freitag, der erste März."**

German, like English, uses ordinal numbers in dates. Add **-te** for the numbers **zwei** to **neunzeh**n, **-ste** for the numbers **zwanzig** and higher. There are three exceptions:

The first of the month is **der erste**.

The third of the month is **der dritte**.

The seventh of the month is **der siebte**.

Germans often write dates in figures followed by a period:

der 14. Juli = der vierzehnte Juli

der 1. März = der erste März

der 20. Mai = der zwanzigste Mai

If you want to express "on July fourteenth" in German, say **"am vierzehnten Juli."** Notice that an **n** is added to the number.

Now, your teacher will divide the class into small groups. Each of you will choose your birthday month and make up a calendar for that month. Complete the calendar with the days of the week and the month in German and enter the dates.

➡ Point to the classroom calendar or sketch one on the chalkboard. Point to a date and say, for example, **"Heute ist Montag, der achte Oktober."** Call on students to identify other dates on the calendar.

➡ Now that students are able to say the date in German, at the beginning of each class period, have a student greet the class, say the date, and write it on the chalkboard. The student says, for example, **"Guten Tag! Heute ist Dienstag, der vierte März."**

➡ Divide the class into groups of three and have each student fill in the month, days, and dates of the blank calendars to reflect the month of her or his birthday this year. Group members then take turns choosing different dates and telling them to one another.

➡ Model **Mein Geburtstag ist am** . . . for students.

Sample Answers to Übung

DEZEMBER						
MONTAG	DIENSTAG	MITTWOCH	DONNERSTAG	FREITAG	SAMSTAG	SONNTAG
1	2	3	4	5	6	7
8	9	10	11	12	13	14
15	16	17	18	19	20	21
22	23	24	25	26	27	28
29	30	31				

➡ *Udo's clues:* Model pronunciation of the German **au, ai, ei,** and **eu** sounds for students. You may wish to refer students to the list of names on page 11 to find and pronounce additional words containing these sounds.

MONTAG						**SONNTAG**

Now that you have completed your calendar, take turns pointing to several dates and saying them to your partners. Then point to the date of your birthdate and say: **Mein Geburtstag ist am** *(My birthday is [on])* . . . followed by the date, with the number ending in **n**.

Udo's clues:

au = ou in house

ai, ei = i in high

eu = oy in boy

Haus, braun

Mai, drei

heute, neun

* German nouns, or names of objects, are masculine, feminine, or neuter. German has two words meaning *a, an:* **ein** is used with masculine and neuter nouns and **eine** is used with feminine nouns.

➡ Linking Dialog 2 and Section 7, "The Classroom"

Dialog 2 and Section 7 will be most effective if treated as a unit. Students need to know the names of two or three classroom objects in order to do the exercise that accompanies the dialog, and they need phrases and expressions of the dialog to discuss objects in the classroom. Students will easily learn the new words **(eine Schülerin, ein Cola)** illustrated in Dialog 2. You could choose one or two additional objects for the activity, then use the new phrases students have just learned as they practice the vocabulary in Section 7.

➡ Before students are asked to read Dialog 2 for meaning, have them look at the characters and guess what Hans and Karin may be saying to each other in each illustration.

➡ Next, model pronunciation either by reading aloud or by playing the cassette while students read the dialog.

➡ Point out and explain informal usage of **Tag!** compared with more formal **Guten Tag!**

➡ Have students close their books. If you have been using "backward build-up," shown on page 13, vary your approach by having students repeat directly from the cassette.

➡ Ask questions such as:

- ◆ How does Karin ask Hans how he is?
- ◆ How does Hans answer?
- ◆ What do you think **Sehr gut** means?
- ◆ What does **danke** mean?
- ◆ What is Hans drawing? What is it called in German?
- ◆ What is Karin holding? What is it called in German?
- ◆ How does Hans ask "What is this?"
- ◆ What does Karin answer?
- ◆ How does Hans say "Thank you"?
- ◆ How does Karin say "You're welcome"?

➡ Greet several students with **"(Guten) Tag,"** allowing them time to respond. Follow immediately with **"Wie geht's?"** and **"Sehr gut, danke."**

➡ Display a pencil and say, **"Das ist ein Bleistift."** Have the class repeat. Then say, **"Was ist das?"** The class answers, **"Das ist ein Bleistift."** Say, **"Danke!"** and have students respond with **"Bitteschön!"**

➡ Repeat the exercise with additional classroom items. Give students a chance to ask each other **"Was ist das?"**

➡ Now is a good time to explain that German nouns, or names of objects, are either masculine, feminine, or neuter and that **ein** is used with masculine and neuter nouns and **eine** is used with feminine nouns.

➡ Have students practice in small groups with **Was ist das?, Das ist ein(e) ___, Danke!,** and **Bitteschön!**

➡ Using hand puppets, have two students improvise a skit in front of the class between two people who meet, greet, ask each other to identify several objects in the classroom, and thank each other.

Now let's review what you learned in Dialog 2:

1. Tag, _____ (name)!

2. Wie geht's?

Sehr gut, danke.

3. Was ist das?

Das ist ein(e) _____.

4. Danke.

Bitteschön.

German Holidays

Most legal holidays celebrated in Germany are based on the religious calendar and are similar to holidays we observe in the United States:

Christmas *(Weihnachten)*: The holiday begins with Christmas Eve on December 24 and continues for two days on December 25 and 26. Germans celebrate by exchanging gifts and decorating the Christmas tree *(der Weihnachtsbaum)*. Students enjoy two weeks vacation until after the New Year holiday.

New Year *(Neujahr)*: New Year's Eve is called *Silvester*. As midnight approaches, church bells ring all over Germany.

Carnival *(Karneval)*: This holiday is celebrated mainly in Catholic areas. Cities known for their carnivals are Cologne, Mainz, and Munich, where people dress in costumes, hold parades, and have parties. The Carnival season reaches its high point just before Ash Wednesday, the beginning of Lent.

Kulturwinkel (Supplementary Culture)

➡ Germans place more importance on celebrating birthdays than do Americans. When celebrating a birthday, Germans are expected to throw their own party for friends and family rather than have a party given for them. Coming of age and round-number birthdays—20, 30, 40—are considered particularly important, especially as people get older.

➡ The Christmas season lasts an entire month. The season begins on the night of December 6, when **Saint Nicholas** arrives on a donkey-drawn sled. Children place one of their shoes on the windowsill, hoping to find it filled with goodies. There are festive Christmas markets set up in many town squares. Streets and buildings are decorated with Christmas trees and electric candles. Special cookies are served at Christmas, as well as a cake filled with raisins, nuts, and candied fruit called **Christstollen.** Roast goose is often the main dish of Christmas dinner. The season ends with Epiphany on January 6, the day of the three kings.

➡ The origins of **Carnival,** celebrated in February, date back to ancient pre-Christian times. It has its roots in the superstitious belief that during the change of seasons, evil spirits brought harm. Noise, laughter, dancing, and scary masks and costumes were believed to frighten away evil spirits.

➡ **Oktoberfest,** an annual gigantic Bavarian folk festival in Munich, actually begins in September and ends in early October. Hundreds of people sit at long tables at beer halls or outdoor areas, crowded together, singing, drinking beer, and eating sausages. The festival attracts about seven million visitors each year. In addition, there is a great parade in the streets of Munich with thousands of people dressed in folk costumes.

➡ During the beginning of fall, groups of children walk with parents or in parades with many other children, carrying candlelit bright paper lanterns, singing songs about the sun, moon, and stars.

➡ On the first day of school, parents give their children large colorful paper cones stuffed with goodies. This is a way to sweeten a child's first day away from home.

Easter *(Ostern)*: The Easter holiday is celebrated for two days. The coloring of Easter eggs, which are then hidden for children to find, is still a popular custom in Germany.

Labor Day *(Tag der Arbeit)*: May 1, formerly celebrated as May Day, is now dedicated to workers, who get a day off from work. Schools, of course, are also closed. In some areas, there are parades and dancing around the maypole.

German Unification Day *(Tag der deutschen Einheit)*: This relatively new holiday celebrates the 1990 unification of West and East Germany on October 3.

Pentecost *(Pfingsten)*: This two-day holiday occurs seven weeks after Easter and is traditionally celebrated with family outings.

Other holidays are celebrated regionally, such as the *Oktoberfest* in Munich, wine festivals in the wine areas along the Rhine and Mosel Rivers, and harvest festivals in many towns and villages throughout Germany.

7 The Classroom

Udo's clues:

The sound of German **ch** does not exist in English. After **a**, **o**, **u**, **au**, pronounce **ch** like *h* in *ahem* when clearing your throat; otherwise, pronounce **ch** like *h* in *hue*.

j = y in yes

acht, Buch, auch   ich, Mädchen, sechzehn   ja, Junge, Juli

Learn the names of the objects in your classroom. See how many names you can remember at a time without having to look at the book.

ein Junge
ein Schüler
ein Stuhl
ein Heft
ein Kugelschreiber
ein Buch

NOTE TO TEACHERS

➡ *Udo's clues:* Model pronunciation of the German **ch** and **j** sounds for students. You may wish to refer students to the list of names on page 11 or cognates on pages 8 and 9 to find and pronounce additional words containing these sounds.

➡ Model pronunciation of classroom words or have students listen to the cassette, allowing time for repetition.

   ◆ Now point to a desk and say, **"Das ist ein Lehrertisch."** Have the class repeat.

   ◆ Indicate a piece of chalk: **"Das ist ein Stück Kreide."**

   ◆ Silently point to the first object, allowing students time to recall and repeat its name.

   ◆ Name a third object, then have the class recall previous objects named.

   ◆ Continue adding items and repeating previously mentioned ones, stretching students' memories.

➡ Use picture dictation for additional reinforcement. Have students draw the object they hear.

➡ A bingo game can easily be adapted as a listening comprehension activity for classroom objects. Draw ten objects on the chalkboard. Name the objects or have students name them. Ask students to pick five of the ten objects and draw them on a piece of paper. Then you name the objects at random as students check if the objects are among those on their papers. The first student to cross out all five objects is the winner.

Note to Teachers

➡ Here is a simple song students will enjoy to practice classroom words. Have students form a circle. One student plays the teacher and steps inside the circle. Another student, blindfolded, tries to find the classmate who is moving in the circle. For classroom objects, a student may hold the object or it may be placed inside the circle on the floor for the blindfolded child to find.

Wo ist . . . ?

1. Wo 'st der Leh - rer? Wo 'st der Leh - rer? Wo, wo, wo? Wo, wo, wo?

Wo wo ist der Leh - rer? Wo wo ist der Leh - rer? Oh, oh, oh! Wo, wo, wo?

2. Heiß, heiß, kalt, kalt, heiß, heiß, kalt, kalt, ganz ganz heiß, ganz ganz kalt.
   Wo, wo ist der Lehrer? Wo, wo ist der Lehrer? Oh, oh, oh! Wo, wo, wo?
3. Wo ist die Tafel? . . .
4. Wo ist der Schüler? . . .
5. Wo ist die Kreide? . . .
6. Wo ist das Mädchen? . . .
7. Wo ist der Kugelschreiber? . . .

© 1994, Uwe Kind

Translation   *WHERE IS . . .?*

  1. Where's the teacher? Where's the teacher? Where, where, where? Where, where, where?
     Where, where's the teacher? Where, where's the teacher? Oh, oh, oh! Where, where, where?

  2. Hot, hot, cold, cold, hot, hot, cold, cold, very very hot, very very cold.
     Where where's the teacher? Where where's the teacher? Where, where, where? Oh, oh, oh!

  3. Where's the chalkboard? . . .

  4. Where's the pupil? . . .

  5. Where's the chalk? . . .

  6. Where's the girl? . . .

  7. Where's the pen? . . .

eine Tafel

ein Fenster

eine Lehrerin

ein Stück Kreide

ein Lehrer

eine Tür

ein Papier

ein Mädchen
eine Schülerin

ein Tisch

ein Bleistift

ein Lehrertisch

The Classroom **37**

ÜBUNG

1. Name aloud as many of the classroom words in German as you can remember. Study the words you did not remember.

2. Write the names of the illustrations in German in the first column of blank lines.

3. Correct your work. Give yourself one point for each correct answer.

4. Now cover the illustrations and write the English meanings of the German words in the second column of blank lines.

5. Correct your work. Give yourself one point for each correct answer.

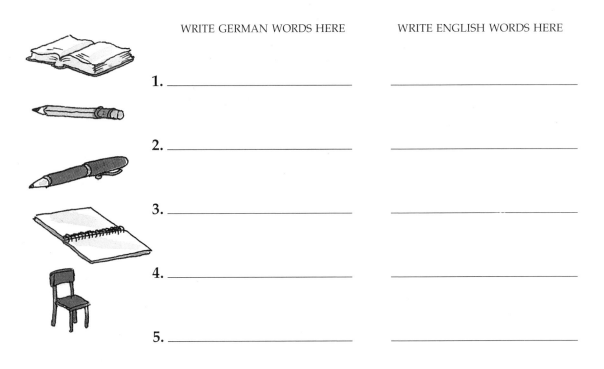

WRITE GERMAN WORDS HERE   WRITE ENGLISH WORDS HERE

1. _____   _____

2. _____   _____

3. _____   _____

4. _____   _____

5. _____   _____

NOTE TO TEACHERS

This activity may be done in class or at home. If done in class, allow time for students to correct their work.

ANSWERS TO ÜBUNG

1. *ein Buch*   *a book*
2. *ein Bleistift*   *a pencil*
3. *ein Kugelschreiber*   *a ballpoint pen*
4. *ein Heft*   *a notebook*
5. *ein Stuhl*   *a chair*

ANSWERS TO ÜBUNG *(continued)*

6. *eine Tafel*   *a chalkboard*

7. *ein Stück Kreide*   *a piece of chalk*

8. *eine Tür*   *a door*

9. *ein Fenster*   *a window*

10. *ein Papier*   *a sheet of paper*

11. *ein Schüler / ein Junge*   *a student / a boy*

12. *eine Schülerin / ein Mädchen*   *a student / a girl*

13. *ein Tisch*   *a student's desk*

14. *ein Lehrertisch*   *a teacher's desk*

15. *ein Lehrer*   *a male teacher*

16. *eine Lehrerin*   *a female teacher*

WRITE GERMAN WORDS HERE   WRITE ENGLISH WORDS HERE

6. _____   _____

7. _____   _____

8. _____   _____

9. _____   _____

10. _____   _____

11. _____   _____

12. _____   _____

13. _____   _____

14. _____   _____

15. _____   _____

16. _____   _____

Thirty-two points is a perfect score. If you made a mistake, you
can improve your score by repeating the exercise on a blank
piece of paper and correcting it again.

Classroom Vocabulary Puzzle: To solve this puzzle, first express the following words in German, then fit them in the puzzle vertically and horizontally:

3-letter word

door   __ __ __

4-letter words

book   __ __ __ __

notebook   __ __ __ __

5-letter words

chalkboard __ __ __ __ __

chair   __ __ __ __ __

boy   __ __ __ __ __

6-letter words

chalk   __ __ __ __ __ __

paper   __ __ __ __ __ __

7-letter words

girl   __ __ __ __ __ __ __

window   __ __ __ __ __ __ __

8-letter word

female teacher __ __ __ __ __ __ __ __

9-letter word

pencil   __ __ __ __ __ __ __ __ __

11-letter word

teacher's desk __ __ __ __ __ __ __ __ __ __ __

14-letter word

pen   __ __ __ __ __ __ __ __ __ __ __ __ __ __

ANSWERS TO ÜBUNG

3-letter word

door   **TÜR**

4-letter words

book   **BUCH**

notebook   **HEFT**

5-letter words

chalkboard   **TAFEL**

chair   **STUHL**

boy   **JUNGE**

6-letter words

chalk   **KREIDE**

paper   **PAPIER**

7-letter words

girl   **MÄDCHEN**

window   **FENSTER**

8-letter word

female teacher   **LEHRERIN**

9-letter word

pencil   **BLEISTIFT**

11-letter word

teacher's desk   **LEHRERTISCH**

14-letter word

pen   **KUGELSCHREIBER**

ANSWERS TO ÜBUNG *(continued)*

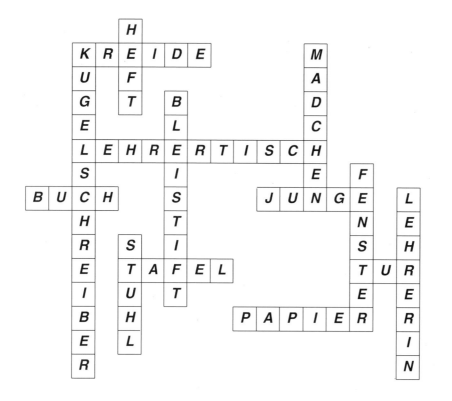

Kulturwinkel

School and Leisure Time

Every German youngster attends kindergarten and then primary school for the first four grades. Starting with the fifth grade, German students can choose to attend different types of secondary schools leading either to academic or vocational studies. At the end of their studies, students must pass a special test to qualify for a place in the university.

German students attend school from Monday to Friday and in some schools on one Saturday a month. Most students take about a dozen subjects at a time, although, of course, not every subject is scheduled every day.

There are about six weeks of summer vacation. Vacation times are staggered in different states of the country to avoid excessive congestion on the highways. Schools are also closed for two to three weeks during the Christmas-New Year season and in the spring.

Young Germans enjoy many of the same leisure activities as their contemporaries in the United States: sports (soccer is by far the most popular sport in Germany), movies, music, arts and crafts, and above all family and school excursions. Germans are passionate travelers and can be seen in large numbers at all the popular travel spots, both in Germany itself as well as throughout Europe and more distant foreign countries.

1. Which classes, sports, and leisure activities are you involved in this year?

_____

2. Do you participate in group excursions? If yes, where did you go this year?

_____

_____

Kulturwinkel (Supplementary Culture)

➡ Most young Germans belong to a local youth group, called a **Verein,** where cultural activities, a variety of courses, and sports are offered. These groups are very popular since schools do not provide any extracurricular activities.

➡ Germans love the outdoors. Hiking, cycling, and camping are very popular in the many nature preserves of the country. Youth hostels provide inexpensive food and lodging for young hikers and bikers traveling across the country. In addition, youth hostels offer a variety of educational programs and excursions. During the school year, schools sometimes participate in nature-study field trips organized by the youth hostels. There are about 500 youth hostels in Germany, 100 in Austria, and 75 in Switzerland.

➡ Teenagers under the age of sixteen are not permitted in bars or discos unless accompanied by an adult. The German Youth Protection Law allows police officers to check young people's ID cards, which they are expected to carry at all times.

➡ You may wish to point out that Germans are enthusiastic gardeners. More than half of all households have a garden they tend with loving care. Sometimes apartment dwellers care for small private gardens grouped together in plots on the edge of towns. In apartment houses, most balconies and windows are adorned with a multitude of plants, providing color and beauty to the urban landscape.

➡ *Udo's clues:* Model pronunciation of German **sch, st,** and **z** sounds for students. You may wish students to find and pronounce additional words containing these sounds in previously learned vocabulary: names, page 11; numbers, page 16; days of the week, page 22; classroom objects, page 36; and colors, page 43.

➡ Model pronunciation of color words or have students listen to the cassette, allowing time for repetition. To teach colors, use crayons, paints, balloons, construction paper, and so on.

➡ Here is a song students will enjoy to practice colors. Repeat both verses using different colors and classroom items.

Alles ist blau

1. Al - les was ich hab' ist blau, blau, blau, blau, blau, blau, blau.

Al - les was ich hab' ist blau, denn ich lie - be blau.

2. Mein Tisch, mein Stuhl, mein Heft sind blau, blau, blau, blau, blau, blau, blau.
   Mein Tisch, mein Stuhl, mein Heft sind blau, denn ich liebe blau.

© 1994, Uwe Kind

Translation

ALL IS BLUE

1. *All I have is blue, blue, blue, blue, blue, blue, blue.*
   All I have is blue, for I love blue.

2. *My table, my chair, my notebook are blue, blue, blue, blue, blue, blue, blue.*
   My table, my chair, my notebook are blue, for I love blue.

8 Colors

Udo's clues:

sch = sh in shoe
st = sht in fishtank

schwarz **St**uhl

z = ts in cats

zehn

gelb
orange
grün
rot
schwarz
blau
weiß
lila
rosa
braun

How many German color words can you memorize in one minute?
Two minutes? Five? When you feel ready, test yourself:

1. Say as many German color words as you can remember.

2. Write the German color words in the first column of blank lines.

3. Check your work and give yourself one point for each correct answer.

4. Now cover the colors and write the English meanings of the German color words in the second column of blank lines.

5. Check your work and give yourself one point for each correct answer.

WRITE GERMAN WORDS HERE   WRITE ENGLISH WORDS HERE

1. _____   _____

2. _____   _____

3. _____   _____

4. _____   _____

5. _____   _____

6. _____   _____

7. _____   _____

8. _____   _____

9. _____   _____

10. _____   _____

Did you get 20 points? If not, try again with a blank piece of paper.

The activity may be done in class or as homework.

ANSWERS TO ÜBUNG

1. *rot* — *red*
2. *orange* — *orange*
3. *gelb* — *yellow*
4. *grün* — *green*
5. *blau* — *blue*
6. *lila* — *purple*
7. *rosa* — *pink*
8. *weiß* — *white*
9. *braun* — *brown*
10. *schwarz* — *black*

➡ This activity associates nouns with adjectives. To enable students to make meaningful combinations, have them learn definite articles of nouns at this point. Having previously learned **ein** and **eine** and the concept of gender, the addition of **der, die,** and **das** follows logically. You may point out that **der, die, das** are the singular articles, there is another article for the plural, **die.**

➡ Some students may ask how to tell the gender of a German noun. Since there are no simple formulas at this level, you may wish to suggest that students memorize the article along with each noun they learn.

Here are pictures of items for which you have already learned the German names:

You already know the INDEFINITE articles *(a, an)* for these nouns: **ein Bleistift, eine Tür, ein Buch.** Now you are ready to learn the DEFINITE articles for the same nouns. Remember that some nouns are masculine, some are feminine, and some are neuter. German has three articles meaning *the*:

masculine = **der (der Bleistift)**   feminine = **die (die Tür)**

neuter = **das (das Buch)**

Find the objects described below in the picture above and color them according to the color indicated. Since you have to know the name of the object *and* the color, give yourself two points for each object you color correctly. You can earn a total of twenty points:

Der Tisch ist braun.   Der Bleistift ist gelb.

Der Stuhl ist rot.   Das Buch ist orange.

Das Papier ist blau.   Das Heft ist lila.

Die Tafel ist schwarz.   Die Kreide ist weiß.

Die Tür ist grün.   Der Kugelschreiber ist rosa.

You've already seen this map. Color the countries where German is spoken according to the colors below:

Germany — **gelb**   Austria — **rot**

Switzerland — **blau**   Liechtenstein — **grün**

Luxemburg — **braun**

NOTE TO TEACHERS

➡ Have students also name the countries where German is spoken.

➡ As a research project, you may wish students to find the colors of the flags of the German-speaking countries. Have students draw, color, and name the colors of the flags. As a class activity, have students collaborate on a color poster of a map and the flags of the German-speaking countries.

➡ Here are the colors of the flags of German-speaking countries:

Austria: red, white, and red, with black eagle

Germany: yellow, red, and black

Liechtenstein: red and blue, with yellow crown

Luxemburg: blue, white, and red

Switzerland: red with white cross

➡ *Udo's clues:* Model pronunciation of words ending with consonant. For additional practice, have students find words ending with consonant in vocabulary already learned: names, page 11; numbers, page 16; days of the week, page 22; classroom objects, page 36; and colors, page 43.

➡ Use picture dictation for additional reinforcement. Have students draw the part of the body they hear.

➡ A bingo game can easily be adapted as a listening comprehension activity for parts of the body vocabulary. Follow the instructions for a similar activity on page 36.

9 The Body

Final **b** is pronounced like *p*, final **d** like *t*, and final **g** like *k*.

final **b, d, g**

gel**b**   Mun**d**   Ta**g**

der Kopf

das Auge
die Nase

die Hand

das Ohr

der Mund

der Arm

When you want to talk about yourself in German, you will need to know the names of the parts of the body. How many names can you remember without having to look at the book?

das Bein

der Fuß

Fill in the names of the parts of the body:

Choose a partner. Point to each other's hand, foot, and so on, and ask, **"Was ist das?"** Answer, **"Das ist eine Hand,"** **"Das ist ein Bein"** (or **"Das ist die Hand,"** **"Das ist das Bein"**) and so on.

ANSWERS TO ÜBUNG

head	*das Auge*	eye	*der Kopf*
ear	*das Ohr*	nose	*die Nase*
mouth	*der Mund*	hand	*die Hand*
arm	*der Arm*	foot	*der Fuß*
leg	*das Bein*		

NOTE TO TEACHERS

➡ Model the second **Übung** with a student in front of the class.

➡ Here is a song children will enjoy to practice words for parts of the body. Have children accompany lyrics with gestures whenever possible.

Die Nase Wackelt

1. Die Na - se wa - ckelt und das rech - te Ohr.

   Die Na - se wa - ckelt und das lin - ke Ohr.

2. Der Mund ist auf, der Mund ist zu.
   Die Hand ist auf dem rechten Schuh.

3. Der Kopf dreht sich im Kreis herum.
   Die Arme hängen locker um.

4. Der Mund ist auf, der Mund ist zu.
   Die Hand ist auf dem linken Schuh.

5. Die Augen auf, die Augen zu.
   Die Hand ist auf dem linken Schuh.

6. Die Augen auf, die Augen zu.
   Die Hand ist auf dem rechten Schuh.

© 1994, Uwe Kind

Translation   THE NOSE WIGGLES

1. The nose wiggles and the right ear.
   The nose wiggles and the left ear.

2. The mouth is open, the mouth is closed.
   The hand's on the right shoe.

3. The head moves around in a circle.
   The arms hang around loosely.

4. The mouth is open, the mouth is closed.
   The hand's on the left shoe.

5. The eyes are open, the eyes are closed.
   The hand's on the left shoe. .

6. The eyes are open, the eyes are closed.
   The hand's on the right shoe.

ANSWERS TO ÜBUNG

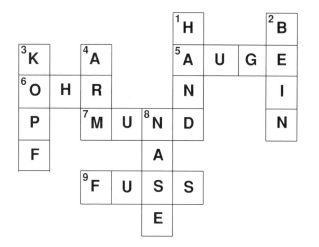

NOTE TO TEACHERS

Simon sagt: One row of students plays while the rest of the class watches to see who makes a mistake and is eliminated. Have students take turns leading each row. If the leader says, **"Simon sagt: ein Mund,"** students should point to their mouth or make it move. If the leader simply says, **"Ein Mund,"** students should remain still. When all rows have played, the winner of each row plays the final round in front of the class.

Complete this crossword puzzle with the German names of the parts of the body (in puzzles using capital letters, ß becomes **SS**):

Across

Down

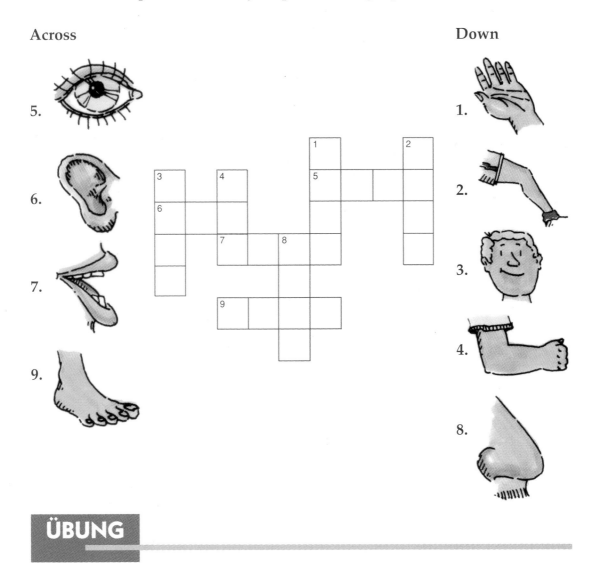

5.

6.

7.

9.

1.

2.

3.

4.

8.

"Simon sagt" means *"Simon says."* Move or point to that part of the body Simon refers to only if you hear the words **"Simon sagt."** If you do not hear the words **"Simon sagt,"** don't move at all.

Some Interesting German Manners and Customs

Germans eat by keeping the fork in the left hand and the knife in the right hand throughout a meal. Eating with knife and fork in this manner is also becoming more prevalent in the United States.

It is customary to bring something for your host or hostess if you're invited to a German home. A box of chocolates or a bouquet of flowers would be just fine. But don't forget to un-wrap the flowers before you present them, for it is considered rude to offer flowers inside wrapping paper.

Germans are much more formal than Americans toward one another. That is why the German language has formal and familiar forms for *you*. Family members, young people, and close friends say **du** to each other, but **Sie** is used for strangers, adults, and business associates. And while your teacher will say **du** to you (at least until you get to high school), good manners require that you address your teacher with **Sie**. A good rule to follow: When in doubt, use **Sie**.

Kulturwinkel (Supplementary Culture)

More German manners and customs:

➡ In restaurants, when a free table is not available, it is common for Germans to share a table with other diners, of course asking permission before joining the table. They may or may not talk with one another, but, before starting to eat, they will politely wish one another **"Guten Appetit,"** roughly *"Enjoy the meal."*

➡ Germans place great importance on courtesy and manners. Being polite in Germany means using a lot of standard expressions: **Ja, bitte** *(Yes, thank you)*, **Nein, danke** *(No, thank you),* **Bitte sehr** when holding the door open or handing something to someone. However, when paid a compliment, Germans do not say "Thank you" as in the U.S.; they simply smile. Germans also stress punctuality, and lateness is considered very bad manners.

➡ Generally, restaurants include a 15 percent tip for service in their prices. Although an extra tip is not necessary, most Germans leave something extra to round off the bill.

➡ Although the American Fahrenheit temperature scale was developed by a German physicist, Germans, like most Europeans, use the Celsius scale. For example, 32° Fahrenheit equals 0° Celsius.

- ◆ To convert Fahrenheit to Celsius, subtract 32 from the Fahrenheit reading, multiply by 5, and divide by 9:

$$45°F = 45 - 32 \times 5 \div 9 = 5°C$$

- ◆ To change Celsius to Fahrenheit, multiply the Celsius reading by 9, divide by 5, and add 32:

$$20°C = 20 \times 9 \div 5 + 32 = 68°F$$

Kulturwinkel (Supplementary Culture)

➡ In addition to supermarkets, small shops play an important role in Germany, especially in towns and villages. Germans prefer the small, individualized neighborhood stores, where they can be sure of the quality and freshness of the products they buy.

➡ There are also open-air markets all over Germany, held once or twice a week that sell all sorts of fresh foods as well as many practical products, clothing, and household equipment. Each town has fixed market days.

➡ The Germans use the metric system for measuring and weighing:

1 **Kilogramm** (1000 grams)	= 2.2 pounds
1 **Pfund**	= 1.1 pounds
1 **Liter**	= 1.06 quarts

➡ Though they share the same language, the German-speaking countries do not share the same currency. The monetary unit of Germany is the Mark (DM); Austria, the Schilling (S); Switzerland and Liechtenstein, the Swiss Franc (sFr).

➡ Advertisements are common in Germany in magazines, billboards, and on television. However, there is one difference: No commercials interrupt German TV programs. Commercials are grouped together and shown at the beginning of the evening's programs (at 8 P.M. and never on Sundays). In addition, German TV's major source of income is a monthly fee that each set owner pays.

Floors in German buildings are numbered beginning with the floor ABOVE the ground floor: **der erste Stock** (first floor) is our second floor, **der zweite Stock** (second floor) is our third floor, and so on. Keep these differences in mind when you shop in a German department store. The ground floor is called **das Erdgeschoß** (literally, earth floor).

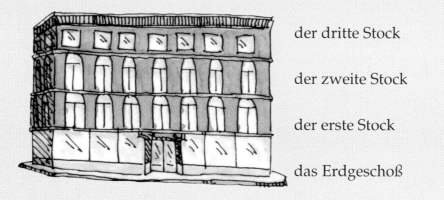

der dritte Stock

der zweite Stock

der erste Stock

das Erdgeschoß

Speaking of shopping in Germany, expect to see labels like these:

These labels look a little strange because Germans use a comma where Americans use a decimal point. As you might have guessed, the reverse is also true: Germans use a decimal point where Americans use a comma:

(Germany) **2.350,25** = (U.S.A.) **2,350.25**

While Americans in general do their grocery shopping once a week, many Germans prefer to buy fresh meats, produce, and baked goods every day for their meals. By the way, the main meal in Germany is still usually eaten at midday.

Talking About Yourself

10

Udo's clue:

ig = ich

traur**ig**, zwanz**ig**

An adjective describes a person or thing. In the sentence "The beautiful girl is happy," *beautiful* and *happy* are adjectives that describe *girl*. Many adjectives are easy to remember if you think of them in pairs:

dünn   **dick**   **intelligent**   **dumm**

traurig   **glücklich**   **klein**   **groß**

schön   **häßlich**   **stark**   **schwach**

➡ *Udo's clue:* Model pronunciation of German words ending in **-ig.** For additional practice, have students find words ending in **-ig** in vocabulary already learned.

➡ Model pronunciation of adjectives or have students listen to the cassette, allowing time for repetition. To teach adjectives, have a student mime adjectives while the class tries to guess the adjective being acted out.

➡ Have students find cognates among the adjectives. Point out any they miss: **intelligent, dumm, groß.** Explain that **stark** and **groß** have different meanings in German.

➡ Here is a song children will enjoy to practice family words. Have children accompany lyrics with gestures whenever possible. For the second verse, have children make a circle. One child mimics a cow, steps into the middle of the circle, points to a classmate, and sings: **"Muuuh, wie geht es dir? Ich heiß' Lu. Wie heißt du?"** The classmate responds with his/her name, then steps into the circle, and the round starts over again. You may wish to repeat with verses three and four. Note: Translation on page 53.

Mein Mutter fliegt ein Jumbojet

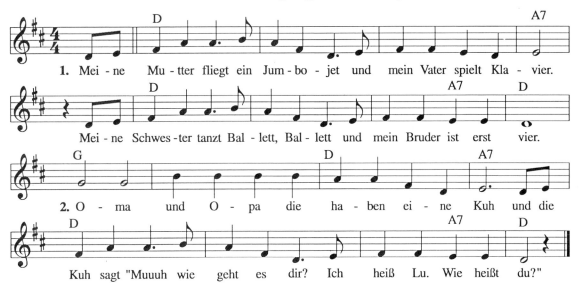

1. Mei - ne Mu - tter fliegt ein Jum - bo - jet und mein Vater spielt Kla - vier.

Mei - ne Schwes - ter tanzt Bal - lett, Bal - lett und mein Bruder ist erst vier.

2. O - ma und O - pa die ha - ben ei - ne Kuh und die

Kuh sagt "Muuuh wie geht es dir? Ich heiß Lu. Wie heißt du?"

3. Oma und Opa die haben eine Kuh, und die
   Kuh sagt "Muuuh, ich trink gern Milchshake, Sag mir, was trinkst du?"
4. Oma und Opa die haben eine Kuh, und die
   Kuh sagt, "Muuuh, ich komm' aus Bern' und woher kommst du?"

1. *My mother flies a jumbo jet and my father plays the piano.*
   My sister dances ballet, ballet, and my brother is just four (years old).

2. *Grandma and Grandpa they have a cow and the*
   cow says "Mooo, how are you? My name is Lou. What's your name?"

3. *Grandma and Grandpa they have a cow, and the*
   cow says "Mooo, I love to drink milk shake, tell me what you're drinking."

4. *Grandma and Grandpa they have a cow and the*
   cow says "I come from Bern, and where do you come from?"

ANSWERS TO ÜBUNG

1. *schön*	2. *häßlich*	3. *traurig*
4. *glücklich*	5. *stark*	6. *schwach*
7. *dünn*	8. *dick*	9. *klein*
10. *groß*	11. *intelligent*	12. *dumm*

NOTE TO TEACHERS

➡ When students have completed this activity, you may ask them to name as well as describe the objects with complete sentences using articles and **ist** *(is)*.

 ◆ **Der Tisch ist braun.**
 ◆ **Die Tafel ist grün.**

Cover page 52 with a sheet of paper and write the German adjectives that describe the objects you see:

1. _____

2. _____

3. _____

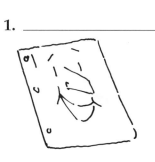

4. _____

5. _____

6. _____

7. _____

8. _____

9. _____

10. _____

11. _____

12. _____

NOTE TO TEACHERS

➡ Before students are asked to read Dialog 3 for meaning, have them guess what Hans and Karin may be feeling and saying to each other in each illustration.

➡ Next, model pronunciation either by reading aloud or by playing the cassette while students read the dialog.

➡ Now have students read the dialog for meaning. Point out new words: **auch, aber, warum, denn, jetzt, und.** Refer students to the vocabulary list at the end of the book for words and phrases they do not understand.

➡ Explain that **ich bin** means *I am* and **du bist** means *you are.*

NOTE TO TEACHERS *(Optional Dialog 4, page 55)*

➡ Dialog 4 is provided for teachers who wish to introduce **Sie** and other formal expressions. You may reproduce it for your students. Dialog may be presented at the end of Section 10, "Talking About Yourself."

➡ Before students are asked to read Dialog 4 for meaning, have them scan the dialog for familiar words and expressions and guess the general content of the conversation.

➡ Next, model pronunciation either by reading aloud or by playing the cassette while students read the dialog.

➡ Now have students close their books. Read short segments for students to repeat. Use the "backward buildup" approach.

➡ Ask questions:
- ◆ How do Karin and Hans greet each other in the evening?
- ◆ How does Karin ask "Who's that?"
- ◆ What is the woman's profession?
- ◆ How does Karin ask the woman her name?
- ◆ How does the German teacher ask Karin her name?
- ◆ How do the Germans say, "His name is ____"?
- ◆ How does Hans ask the German teacher how she is?

➡ Point out the difference between formal and informal expressions:

Wie heißen Sie?	**Wie heißt du?**
Wie geht es Ihnen?	**Wie geht's?**
Sie sind . . .	**Du bist . . .**

➡ New vocabulary and expressions:

Guten Abend.	*Good evening.*
Wer ist das?	*Who is that?*
Sie ist Deutschlehrerin.	*That's the German teacher.*
Ich weiß nicht.	*I don't know.*
Wie heißen Sie?	*What's your name? (formal)*
Wie heißt sie?	*What's her name?*
Sie (Er) heißt . . .	*Her (His) name is . . .*
Dies ist . . .	*This is . . .*
Sie sind Deutschlehrerin.	*You are the German teacher. (formal)*
Nicht wahr?	*Right? Isn't that so?*
Wie geht es Ihnen?	*How are you? (formal)*

Dialog 4 (Optional)

Guten Abend

Karin and Hans meet at an international school fair organized by the foreign language department of their school. It is 7:00 P.M.

Karin:	**Guten Abend, Hans.**
Hans:	**Guten Abend, Karin.**

Karin points to a woman.

Karin:	**Wer ist das?**
Hans:	**Sie ist Deutschlehrerin.**
Karin:	**Wie heißt sie?**
Hans:	**Ich weiß nicht.**

Karin walks toward the German teacher.

Karin:	**Guten Abend. Sie sind Deutschlehrerin, nicht wahr?**
Frau Schmidt:	**Ja. Wie heißt du?**
Karin:	**Ich heiße Karin. Und Sie, wie heißen Sie?**
Frau Schmidt:	**Ich heiße Ilse Schmidt.**

Karin and Frau Schmidt shake hands.

Karin:	**Freut mich, Frau Schmidt.**
Frau Schmidt:	**Freut mich, Karin.**

Karin gestures to Hans to join them.

Karin:	**Dies ist Hans.**
Frau Schmidt:	**Guten Abend, Hans. Ich heiße Ilse Schmidt.**
Hans:	**Freut mich, Frau Schmidt. Wie geht es Ihnen?**
Frau Schmidt:	**Danke, sehr gut.**

Let's take a closer look at some of the words you learned in Dialog 3:

Ich bin . . .

Du bist . . .

Er ist . . .
Der Junge ist . . .

Sie ist . . .
Das Mädchen ist . . .

➡ Have the class repeat, "**Ich bin traurig.**" Then say "**dünn.**" The class repeats, "**Ich bin dünn.**"

➡ Continue with **dumm, traurig, schwach,** and **klein.**

➡ Follow the same procedure with **du bist.**

➡ Present **der Junge ist (er ist)** and **das Mädchen ist (sie ist).**

Practice these three forms of **sein** *(to be)* with all the adjectives until the class has mastered them.

➡ You may wish to use picture dictation as a listening comprehension activity to practice **ist** and adjectives as well as reinforce previously learned vocabulary. Have students write and then draw what they hear, for example:

Das Mädchen ist glücklich.   **Der Junge ist traurig.**

Das Buch ist groß.   **Das Heft ist klein.**

Have students check and correct each other's pictures and phrases. You may wish to create a composite poster of student drawings and written descriptions for display in the classroom.

➡ You may wish to practice these forms with photographs, magazine pictures, cartoons, and so on. Have students describe the people in the pictures.

➡ Have students in groups of three or four practice describing one another. Demonstrate with two or three students in front of the class:

Ich bin stark. Du bist auch stark.
Nein, ich bin schwach. Aber ich bin intelligent.

Bist du traurig?
Nein, ich bin glücklich. Und ich bin sehr schön.

➡ You may wish to use this writing activity to review structures and vocabulary learned in this section:

◆ Make a copy of the dialog on pages 54 and 55 and whiten out the text in the bubbles.

◆ Divide the class into groups of two and distribute a dialog to each student.

◆ Have partners create a dialog to be inserted in the empty bubbles. Refer students to the vocabulary list at the end of the book for words and phrases they need.

◆ Circulate among students, advising, correcting, and answering questions.

◆ When dialogs have been completed and corrected, have students memorize them and dramatize them for the class.

ÜBUNG

Your teacher will now divide you into small groups to practice describing yourself and one another.

ÜBUNG

Play charades with the adjectives you have learned. Your teacher will divide the class into teams, and a member from one team will stand in front of the class and act out the various ways he or she would look if sad, intelligent, fat, and so on.

Kulturwinkel

Sports in Germany

Fußball *(Soccer)* is not only the most popular spectator sport in Germany but also the sport that young Germans most actively engage in as soon as they are old enough to kick a soccer ball. Every school and every town has its own soccer team, and the national team is followed by practically every German whenever it plays an international match.

Germans of all ages are also actively engaged in a variety of other individual and team sports: tennis, gymnastics, track and field, swimming, bicycling, and skiing. In recent years, basketball and volleyball have become increasingly popular, but American football and baseball are still relatively rare.

Kulturwinkel (Supplementary Culture)

➡ One third of the German population participates in 63,000 sports clubs of all sorts. Gymnastics, track and field, tennis, swimming, bowling, handball, and table tennis are popular. With the exception of soccer, team sports are not as popular in Germany as in the United States.

➡ The mountains provide opportunities for skiing and mountain climbing. Northern Germany provides fine beaches for swimming and boating.

➡ Many clubs throughout the country plan weekend hikes of different lengths and difficulty. Germans of all ages participate, and sometimes the whole family takes part.

➡ Model pronunciation of family words or have students listen to the cassette, allowing time for repetition.

➡ You may wish to point out the close relationship between **mein/meine, dein/deine** and the indefinite articles **ein/eine.** Because of their common endings, possessives and indefinite articles are often called "**ein**-words."

Kulturwinkel (Supplementary Culture)

➡ You may wish to point out that the family is very important to the Germans. Parents tend to be strict, especially fathers. Obedience, respect, good behavior, and manners are encouraged and expected.

➡ Germans value their privacy; casual visits are unusual and an invitation to someone's home is a special occasion. Most German houses are surrounded by fences and doors are typically kept closed with window curtains drawn at night. Great care is taken to make the home comfortable and attractive. Flowers and plants adorn most window sills and balconies.

➡ Although German people may seem more formal and private than Americans, this should not be mistaken for coldness or distrust. The Germans are a fun-loving people who cherish friendship and good company. For the Germans, personal friendship develops slowly; but once a friend, always a friend.

11 The Family

Here we have a typical German family **(die Familie)**. Let's take a closer look at the family members:

der Sohn, der Bruder
die Großmutter
der Großvater
die Tochter, die Schwester
die Mutter
der Vater

Naturally, German boys and girls also use nicknames for their parents and grandparents:

der Vati = der Vater   **die Mutti = die Mutter**

der Opa = der Großvater   **die Oma = die Großmutter**

If you want to say "my father," "my mother," "your father," "your mother," it's really very simple:

mein Vater   **meine Mutter**

dein Vater   **deine Mutter**

Use **mein / dein** for masculine and **meine / deine** for feminine.

Wer ist das? Identify these members of the family. Use nicknames, if you like. Here's an example:

Das ist die Mutti.

Now it's your turn. **Wer ist das?**

1. _____

2. _____

3. _____

_____

_____

_____

4. _____

5. _____

_____

_____

ANSWERS TO ÜBUNG

1. *Das ist der Sohn.*

2. *Das ist die Großmutter (die Oma).*

3. *Das ist der Vater (der Vati).*

4. *Das ist die Tochter.*

5. *Das ist der Großvater (der Opa).*

NOTE TO TEACHERS

➡ Here is a song students will enjoy to practice adjectives. Have students accompany lyrics with gestures whenever possible.

Der dicke Wal

1. Der dick-e Wal, Ein dick-er Wal, Ich se-he ein-en dick-en Wal.
Ich se-he ein-en dick-en, dick-en, Ich se-he ein-en dick-en Wal.

2. Das alte Haus, Ein altes Haus, Ich wohn' in einem alten Haus.
   Ich wohn' in einem alten, alten, Ich wohn' in einem alten Haus.

3. Die schöne Kuh, Die schöne Kuh, Ich sehe eine schöne Kuh.
   Ich sehe eine schöne, schöne, Ich sehe eine schöne Kuh.

4. Die kleine Maus, Die kleine Maus, Ich sehe eine kleine Maus.
   Ich sehe eine kleine, kleine, Ich sehe eine kleine Maus.

© 1994, Uwe Kind

Translation

THE FAT WHALE

1. *The fat whale, a fat whale, I see a fat whale.*
   I see a fat, fat, I see a fat whale.

2. *The old house, an old house, I live in an old house.*
   I live in an old, old, I live in an old house.

3. *The pretty cow, a pretty cow, I see a pretty cow.*
   I see a pretty, pretty, I see a pretty cow.

4. *The small mouse, a small mouse, I see a small mouse.*
   I see a small, small, I see a small mouse.

ANSWERS TO ÜBUNG

YOU	YOUR PARTNER
1. *Dein Großvater ist klein.*	*Nein, mein Großvater ist groß.*
2. *Deine Schwester ist dick.*	*Nein, meine Schwester ist dünn.*
3. *Deine Mutter ist häßlich.*	*Nein, meine Mutter ist schön.*
4. *Dein Bruder ist schwach.*	*Nein, mein Bruder ist stark.*

Team up with a partner in the following dialog. Make believe that you are describing a member of your partner's family, but your partner responds with the opposite description. Here's an example to get you started:

You	Your Partner

Dein Großvater ist klein.	Nein, mein Großvater ist groß.

1. _____

2. _____

3. _____

4. _____

12 Recycling German

Your teacher will now give you time to use your German. Think of all you have learned!

- ◆ You can say your name!
- ◆ You can count and do math!
- ◆ You can name the days of the week and the months of the year!

- ◆ You can name objects in the classroom with their colors!
- ◆ You can describe yourself and others and point out parts of the body!

When someone asks if you can speak German: **Sprichst du Deutsch?**, now you can answer: **Ja, ich spreche Deutsch!**

ÜBUNG

Fill in the boxes with the German meanings and you will find a mystery word in the longest vertical column. Write the mystery word in German and English in the blanks provided:

1. three
2. Monday
3. January
4. boy
5. desk
6. ear
7. window
8. red
9. thank you
10. pen

NOTE TO TEACHERS

➡ As a culminating activity, give students the opportunity to make an oral presentation on a cultural topic studied. You may wish to divide the class into small groups, with each student contributing to the research of the topic. The group then chooses a representative to speak in front the class.

➡ Now would be a good time to teach **Sprichst du Deutsch?** and **Ja, ich spreche Deutsch.** Give students a chance both to ask and answer the question.

ANSWERS TO ÜBUNG

Mystery word: *Donnerstag*
Thursday

1.			D	R	E	I					
2.		M	O	N	T	A	G				
3.	J	A	N	U	A	R					
4.	J	U	N	G	E						
5.	L	E	H	R	E	R	T	I	S	C	H
6.		O	H	R							
7.	F	E	N	S	T	E	R				
8.	R	O	T								
9.		D	A	N	K	E					
10.	K	U	G	E	L	S	C	H	R	E	I	B	E	R

NOTE TO TEACHERS

➡ Have students correct each other's work as you circulate among the class, checking students' answers.

➡ For additional speaking practice of vocabulary and the verb **sein,** you may wish to have students show their colored monster picture to the class and describe its colors in complete sentences. Students point to a part of the body and say, for example, **"Die Nase ist rot."** or **"Das Auge ist blau."**

Have the class play the role of teacher and correct classmates' errors in German.

ANSWERS TO ÜBUNG *(Colors will vary.)*

1. *der Kopf*

2. *der Mund*

3. *das Auge*

4. *das Ohr*

5. *die Nase*

6. *die Hand*

7. *das Bein*

8. *der Fuß*

9. *der Arm*

Colors: What would this funny monster look like if you could color the parts of its body? Write the names of the parts of the body and the colors you would choose in the blanks below. Then color the parts of the body in the picture:

Part of the body	Color
1. _____	_____
2. _____	_____
3. _____	_____
4. _____	_____
5. _____	_____
6. _____	_____
7. _____	_____
8. _____	_____
9. _____	_____

Can you complete these dialogs or express the following ideas in German?

1. You overhear the conversation of these two people who are meeting for the first time. Complete the dialog:

Sample Answers to Übung

1. Girl: *Tag! Wie heißt du?*

   Boy: *Tag! Ich heiße _____. Und du?*

   Girl: *Ich heiße _____. Freut mich.*

   Boy: *Freut mich auch.*

   Girl: *Wie geht's?*

   Boy: *Ich bin traurig.*

1. Boy: *Auf Wiedersehen, _____!*

   Girl: *Tschüs, _____!*

2. Peter: *Was ist das?*

   Brother: *Das ist ein Buch.*

   Peter: *Was ist das?*

   Brother: *Das ist ein Kugelschreiber?*

2. Peter is teaching some German words to his little brother. Complete the dialog:

3. What do you think these friends are saying to each other?

4. What are the colors of the American flag?

_____   _____   _____

5. What are the names of these parts of the body?

 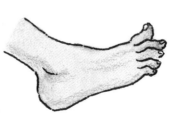 

_____   _____   _____

Sample Answers *(continued)*

3. Girl: *Danke!*

   Boy: *Bitteschön!*

4. *rot*   *weiß*   *blau*

5. *der Mund*   *der Fuß*   *die Hand*

Sample Answers *(continued)*

6.

Januar	
9 Montag	
10 *Dienstag*	
11 Mittwoch	
12 *Donnerstag*	
13 Freitag	
14 *Samstag*	
15 *Sonntag*	

7. *April*   *August*   *Dezember*

8. *schwach*   *dick*   *schön*

6. What days of the week are
missing from this agenda?

7. What month is it?

_____   _____   _____

8. What adjectives describe these people?

_____   _____   _____

This game is played like **Bingo,** except that it is played with words. Select German words from the categories in the vocabulary list on pages 70 to 73 as directed by your teacher. Write one word in each square at random from the chosen categories.

Your teacher will read the **Bingo** words in English. If one of the German words on your card matches the English word you hear, mark that square with a small star. When you have five stars in a row, either horizontally, vertically, or diagonally, call out **"Bingo!"**

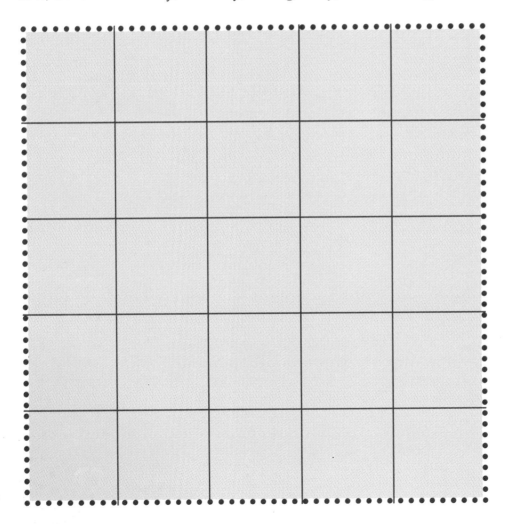

NOTE TO TEACHERS

➡ Choose categories of vocabulary you wish students to review.

➡ Complete a bingo board with 25 words from the chosen categories.

➡ Read or have students take turns reading the words aloud for the class.

➡ Check to see if a word has been spelled correctly before declaring a student a winner.

NOTE TO TEACHERS

➡ As students encountered the German people and their language, they were probably both entertained and impressed by the differences between German and American lifestyles and culture. Now is an excellent time to reinforce respect for both cultures and foster appreciation of cultural differences.

Sample Answers

➡ You may wish to discuss further how Americans generally greet one another. Ask students how they and their parents greet close family members, relatives, good friends, and acquaintances.

GERMAN	AMERICAN
2. *To say "you," young people say "du" to each other and "Sie" to adults.*	*There is only one way to say "you."*
3. *Schools do not organize sport teams or after-school activities.*	*Schools provide many extracurricular activities and sports.*
4. *Soccer is the most popular sport.*	*Football and baseball are the most popular sports.*
5. *The school day ends at 1 P.M. and there are sometimes classes on Saturday.*	*The school day ends at 3 P.M. and there is no school on Saturday.*
6. *One is the highest school grade.*	*100 or A is the highest school grade.*

Hurrah for the differences!

Now that you have learned quite a bit about the German language and about Germany and its people, can you list the differences between Germans and Americans that impressed you the most? Jog your memory by looking over the **Kulturwinkel** on pages 15, 23, 34–35, 42, 50–51, and 58.

An example is given to get you started:

GERMAN	AMERICAN
1. *Friends and relatives greet each other with "Tag" and shake hands.*	*Friends and relatives say "Hi" and may kiss women on the cheek.*
2.	
3.	
4.	
5.	
6.	

Vocabulary

Numbers

eins	1
zwei	2
drei	3
vier	4
fünf	5
sechs	6
sieben	7
acht	8
neun	9
zehn	10
elf	11
zwölf	12
dreizehn	13
vierzehn	14
fünfzehn	15
sechzehn	16
siebzehn	17
achtzehn	18
neunzehn	19
zwanzig	20
einundzwanzig	21
zweiundzwanzig	22
dreiundzwanzig	23
vierundzwanzig	24
fünfundzwanzig	25
sechsundzwanzig	26
siebenundzwanzig	27
achtundzwanzig	28
neunundzwanzig	29
dreißig	30
einunddreißig	31
zweiunddreißig	32
dreiunddreißig	33
vierunddreißig	34
fünfunddreißig	35
sechsunddreißig	36
siebenunddreißig	37
achtunddreißig	38
neununddreißig	39
vierzig	40

Arithmetic

Wie viele?	How many?
ist	equals
und	and, plus
weniger	minus

Days of the week

Montag	Monday
Dienstag	Tuesday
Mittwoch	Wednesday
Donnerstag	Thursday
Freitag	Friday
Samstag	Saturday
Sonntag	Sunday

Months of the year

Januar	January
Februar	February
März	March
April	April
Mai	May
Juni	June
Juli	July
August	August
September	September
Oktober	October
November	November
Dezember	December

The Classroom

ein Bleistift	a pencil
ein Buch	a book
ein Fenster	a window
ein Heft	a notebook
ein Junge	a boy
ein Kugelschreiber	a ballpoint pen
ein Lehrer	a (male) teacher
eine Lehrerin	a (female) teacher
ein Lehrertisch	a (teacher's) desk
ein Mädchen	a girl
ein Papier	a paper
ein Schüler	a (male) student
eine Schülerin	a (female) student
ein Stück Kreide	a piece of chalk
ein Stuhl	a chair
eine Tafel	a chalkboard
ein Tisch	a (student's) desk
eine Tür	a door

Colors

blau	blue
braun	brown
gelb	yellow
grün	green
lila	purple
orange	orange
rosa	pink
rot	red
schwarz	black
weiß	white

The Body

der Arm	the arm
das Auge	the eye
das Bein	the leg
der Fuß	the foot
die Hand	the hand
der Kopf	the head
der Mund	the mouth
die Nase	the nose
das Ohr	the ear

Adjectives

dein, deine	your
dick	fat
dumm	stupid, dumb
dünn	thin
glücklich	happy
groß	big, tall
häßlich	ugly
intelligent	intelligent, smart
klein	small
mein, meine	my
schön	beautiful, handsome
schwach	weak
stark	strong
traurig	sad

The Family

mein, meine	my
dein, deine	your
der Vater, der Vati	the father, the dad
die Mutter, die Mutti	the mother, the mom
der Großvater, der Opa	the grandfather
die Großmutter, die Oma	the grandmother
der Sohn	the son
die Tochter	the daughter
der Bruder	the brother
die Schwester	the sister

Expressions and phrases

Wie heißt du? Wie heißen Sie?	What's your name?
Ich heiße . . .	My name is . . .
Und du?	And you?
Freut mich.	It's a pleasure.
Frau	Mrs., Ms.
Herr	Mister, sir
Tag!	Hi!, Hello! (informal)
Guten Tag!	Hello!, Good day! (formal)
Guten Morgen!	Good morning!
Guten Abend!	Good evening!
Gute Nacht!	Good night!
(Auf) Wiedersehen!	Good-bye!
Tschüs!	Bye-bye!, So long!
Heute ist (date).	Today is (date).
der erste	the first
der dritte	the third
der siebte	the seventh
der vierzehnte	the fourteenth
der zwanzigste	the twentieth
am vierzehnten	on the fourteenth

Mein Geburtstag ist am . . .	My birthday is [on] . . .
Wie geht's?	How are you?
Sehr gut, danke.	Very well, thank you.
Wer ist das?	Who is that?
Was ist das?	What is that?
Das ist ein(e) . . .	That is a (an) . . .
Das ist der (die, das) . . .	That is the . . .
Danke.	Thank you.
Bitteschön.	You're welcome.
Warum?	Why?
das Erdgeschoß	the ground floor
der erste Stock	the first floor
der zweite Stock	the second floor
der dritte Stock	the third floor
Ich bin . . .	I am . . .
Du bist . . .	You are . . .
Er ist . . .	He is . . .
Der Junge ist . . .	The boy is . . .
Sie ist . . .	She is . . .
Das Mädchen ist . . .	The girl is . . .
Sprichst du Deutsch?	Do you speak German?
Ja, ich spreche Deutsch.	Yes, I speak German.
Kulturwinkel	Culture corner
aber	but
auch	also
jetzt	now
und	and
Ja.	Yes.
Nein.	No.